BV
4011
.S58
1988

Brengle Memorial Library
The Salvation Army
School for Officers Training
DISCARD
Suffern, N.Y.

'90-223

THE IMPOSSIBLE VOCATION

JOHN SNOW

is an Episcopal priest and Professor of Pastoral Theology at Episcopal Divinity School and also Preacher-In-Residence at Christ Church in Cambrige, MA. He is author of *Mortal Fear: Meditations on Death and AIDS, On Pilgrimage: Marriage in the Seventies, The Gospel in a Broken World,* and one volume of the *Fortress Proclamation Series.*

THE IMPOSSIBLE VOCATION

Ministry in the Mean Time

JOHN SNOW

COWLEY PUBLICATIONS
CAMBRIDGE, MASSACHUSETTS

©1988 by John Snow. All rights reserved.
Published in the United States of America
by Cowley Publications
International Standard Book No.: 0-936384-58-1

Library of Congress Cataloging-in-Publication Data
Snow, John M., 1924 -
    The impossible vocation.

    Bibliography: p.
    1. Pastoral theology. 2. Clergy—Office.
I. Title.
BV4011.S58   1988   253   88-409
ISBN 0-936384-58-1

Cowley Publications
980 Memorial Drive
Cambridge, MA 02138

ACKNOWLEDGMENTS

I want to acknowledge the intelligent and sustaining help of Paula Wendland as I tried to make these lectures into a book.

For Paul Berg
who brought light to many.

CONTENTS

The Impossible Vocation

I want to begin with a true story. In 1957, my last year in seminary, I was a candidate for ordination in the Diocese of Rhode Island. In the late fall all candidates were invited to attend a diocesan retreat for clergy at which the canon preacher at a major urban cathedral was to be the leader. He was an impressive-looking fellow in his late fifties who at the time was a kind of show piece for the Episcopal Church. He had come late to ordination, a rare thing in those days, after having been a scientist. In a sense, he was the church's "So there!" to science. "You see," his presence seemed to remark, "a highly intelligent man with a scientific background can commit himself to Christianity, can even become an articulate spokesman for Christianity. He can speak both languages. In him we can see the reconciliation of what C.P. Snow called the two cultures."

The retreat was a dud. The canon spoke at a high level of abstraction about something or other, I can't remember what, as the clergy dozed or slipped out for a cigarette or stared at the ceiling. The decade of the fifties had its own kind of parochial stress as the churches filled to overflowing. Many of the clergy were involved in high-pressure building campaigns and their fatigue was obvious.

And then something happened that I remember vividly. The speaker suddenly began to talk about the pressures on the successful corporation executives he worked with. "They look so prosperous, so self-assured, so purposeful," he told us, "but underneath, they're desperate. Do you know that of ten such men I know well, eight have ulcers? We clergy may not make much money or be given much public recognition, but at least we don't have ulcers."

I turned to the priest sitting next to me and whispered, "That's funny. I'm not even ordained yet and I have an ulcer." He winked at me and replied, "So do I." I felt a touch on my shoulder and turned my head. The fellow behind me whispered rather loudly, "I have an ulcer, too." Heads began to nod around us. Finally an older and rather distinguished priest of the diocese interrupted the speaker and said, "Canon, I think you should know that a fair percentage of us here in this room do have ulcers." And that was the end of that retreat. The canon apologized, but there was nothing much more that he could say, and the clergy departed, some of them more angry and depressed than when they arrived.

Those of us who had ulcers were not merely angry, but suffering even more from the loss of self-esteem that ulcers created in those who had them in those days. Parish clergy tend to be the least psychologically naive professionals in their community. We had learned in our Clinical Pastoral Education training as well as in our reading in counseling about the "ulcer personality." We knew that ulcers were supposed to be a psychogenic disease caused by aggression turned inward, and so forth. I really did begin to question whether I should be ordained at all. Could someone with an ulcer really be *called* to ordination? Perhaps I should go into therapy first and clean up my psyche before ordination.

What reassured me was reading a novel by J.D. Salinger called *Franny and Zooey*, in which the hero announces to his mother that he has an ulcer. His mother gets upset and begins to blame herself. He interrupts her and says,

"Look, Mom, anybody over thirty who *doesn't* have an ulcer is a goddamned spy!" I decided to look upon my ulcer as a kind of purple heart, a badge of serious engagement with the world, and proceeded to be ordained.

Five years later, working as a parish minister, I picked up the *New York Times* and discovered that beyond all argument, smoking gave you cancer. Like most clergy at the time, I was a heavy smoker. My attitude towards giving up smoking was the same as Mark Twain's. It was easy. I had done it hundreds of times. Nevertheless, I did give up smoking. And I have never had a twinge from my ulcer since. In fact, there is no ulcer there that an X-ray can discover. My ulcer was not caused by rage turned inward; it was caused by smoking. All the self-doubt, the vocational anxiety, the sense of somehow being marked like Cain had been needless. I was not a walking nut-case after all. I should add here that when the doctor had first diagnosed the ulcer we had discussed giving up smoking. "You can try it," he said, "but it's my opinion that giving up smoking will be so stressful that it will exacerbate the ulcer more than it will help."

This story points up the fact that living in a society which has wholeheartedly adopted the language and assumptions of therapeutic practice is confusing. The whole reason for adopting therapeutic values is to remove blame from human interaction, so that human beings can look objectively at their behavior and its motivation and alter it to reduce conflict and suffering. In a sense, "therapeutic values" is a contradiction in terms, since therapy for years claimed to be value-free, like science. Yet within therapy objectivity is a high value and a subjective therapist is quickly blamed. Indeed, the language of therapy can be used to blame as easily as it can be used to describe. There may no longer be such a thing as a bad boy, as Father Flannagan of Boys' Town used to say, but you can say, "Wow, is that kid *sick!*" and mean roughly the same thing.

By the mid-fifties the word "sick" was becoming something of an epithet. Even pastors, faced with parishioners' resistance to building programs or liturgical change, tended to see whoever generated the resistance as "excessively rigid" or "having authority problems" or, in extreme cases, "suffering from an unresolved Oedipus complex." The most usual put-down was, "You know Jim. Some problems there." The simple, ill-defined concept of "problems" was more destructive of another's credibility and general trustworthiness than being called a son-of-a-bitch. "Problems" assumed pathology, that a person's behavior was a result of an imperfect upbringing and hence beyond control. Unless of course the person with problems opted for "skilled counseling."

In a real way, the use of therapeutic concepts in normal parish interaction (fund-raising, recruiting church school teachers, planning an Every Member Canvas) is where therapeutic assumptions about human nature entered into the general moral environment of the parish. Formerly when we claimed that someone resisting change in the parish was mistaken, stubborn, old-fashioned or even "bad," with its many metaphors and nuances, we assumed a cognitive conflict and a conscious commitment on the part of the resister to an idea, an apprehension of reality that made sense to them. We assumed also that since the idea was conscious, it could be met with something closer to the truth, or more moral, and thus changed. However there is little point in trying to use logic or persuasion on someone who has "problems," to say nothing of the group of "neurotics" who surround this person in the parish. One might assume that her "resistance" was due to feeling insecure, not a "part" of the parish, and arrange to get her on this or that parish committee in order to make her "feel wanted." Or one could ignore people with problems altogether; they were clearly outside the larger parish consensus and no threat to the accomplishment of whatever task one was intent on doing.

In the churches' slow assimilation of therapeutic assumptions, a shift also occurred in the doctrine of freedom of the will. It moved from a perhaps too high, almost Pelagian doctrine— where everyone is free to deal consciously with reality if that is what they intend to do— to a low Augustinian or Calvinist doctrine where some are God's (or Nature's) elect and some are not. Some are healthy, that is, and some are sick. Some have a strong ego; some are at the mercy of their unconscious, creatures of unconscious inhibition or impulse. There is, of course, a therapeutic model for good behavior: it is adaptive behavior. But therapy has little to say about what we are supposed to adapt to. That is a value question and different for different people. You can say that people can adapt to "reality," but lately there is a tendency to believe that the concept of reality itself is an oppressive trip laid on us by whoever is in power at the moment. "Look, Jones," the corporate vice president says to the obstreperous junior manager, "when are you going to face reality?" According to this school, everyone has a right to his or her own reality. Like the back ward of a mental hospital, or more recently, like a city street, full of people nursing their own realities.

The top value, the most inclusive and persuasive value in a therapeutic culture, is pluralism. For pluralism, ideas are less important than a society free of conflict. Give everyone space for his or her ideas about reality, and we will live happily together. The trouble here, I suspect, is that human behavior is not simply a matter of motivation, but also a matter of purpose. People are not just driven by what happened to them in the past, they are also drawn into the future by purpose, by vision. Ideas that are truly ideas lead inevitably to purpose; different ideas lead to different purposes.

Pluralism is such an idea. Its purpose is a pluralistic society. In the matter of abortion, we can see this clearly. Those who regard themselves as pro-choice tend to be pluralists. If women are opposed to abortion, let them bear children. We want a society where women may choose what to do about their own bodies and the government does not interfere. But those who think of themselves as pro-life have a different purpose entirely. They want a society that legally enforces a consensus based on beliefs about good and evil. They have a different idea. These ideas, because they don't share the same teleology, the same purpose, the same end, do not coexist happily.

Yet they coexist willy-nilly, or the more passionate ideologies go into schism and make ideology into a new religion. In so many cases the parish minister is faced with a parish which contains not only single-issue cliques, but also the wider division between pluralists and what might be called nostalgic moralists—people who want to recapture a moral consensus which they believe they knew in their own lifetime. Nostalgic moralists rightly see a "breakdown in moral values" and find the discontinuity in customary corporate behavior painful and socially destructive. They see pluralism as a blessing of this discontinuity and hence an evil thing.

Pluralists, on the other hand, see the breakdown of the rigidities of a moral code designed for earlier times as a good and liberating thing. They do, however, bless pluralism as a social goal, a kind of vision of the holy city, only imperfectly realized so far, but the ideal toward which Christians, along with the rest of the world, should strive in their corporate life. The means by which Christian pluralists would achieve their vision are based largely on therapeutic assumptions, not the least important of which is that ongoing conflict, consciously experienced as suffering, is maladaptive. They tend to see their adversaries in the parish (people who, in their view, "have a perfect right to their ideas, but not to forcing them on us") as having problems.

The purpose of this book is to examine the failure of moral consensus that is currently creating considerable turbulence in parish life. Don Browning, Robert Bellah, Alasdair MacIntyre and others are all insisting on the need for some sort of moral consensus for a viably human corporate life; both Browning and Bellah see the parish church as a likely place to begin to reconstruct it. It is my view that if Christians can come to understand pluralism as the most humane alternative for an interim period of moral ambiguity and anxiety between two moral paradigms, one aging and parlous, the other only beginning to be born, then the church can concern itself with the enormously difficult task of building a new moral consensus. For this to happen, Christians will have to take their baptism very seriously indeed. It will mean coexistence, conversation between conflicting ideologies, and theological interpretation of Scripture within the church in an atmosphere of high seriousness, not easy tolerance. Yet this would seem a more appropriate approach to the turmoil and conflict plaguing our parishes today than the facile manipulations of low-profile crisis management and conflict resolution by professionalized pastors. A congregation where many members have quite idiosyncratic ideas about the purpose of the parish, or even of Christianity itself, presents a dilemma which skills in crisis management are not likely to remove.

In some respects the insights of therapy have helped make possible a creative interim period between moral paradigms, and it is helpful in trying to address this issue to look at the short-term history of how the therapeutic metaphor has penetrated the mind of the church and its ministers. In doing this I will use at different times the terms priest, pastor, and parish minister, but in all cases I am referring to ordained ministers. Writing as an Episcopalian, I mean by priest someone whose role is more traditionally, canonically, symbolically and hierarchically defined than the traditional Protestant pastor's, but in practice not radically different. Priesthood, as I intend it here, is a somewhat more vivid caricature of what it is to be a pastor; to a degree it is more sharply set off from the laity by symbols of the office and by canon law. The most significant difference between priest and people lies in the priest alone being permitted by the church to celebrate the Eucharist.

Now I want to move from the culture in general to the parish in particular, and do it with a brief history of pastoral counseling. First I will say something about the theological experience of mainline seminarians for a decade or so after World War II that left them so open to therapeutic theory as a world view. When I went to seminary in the fifties, the most influential theologians in America were Reinhold Niebuhr, Paul Tillich, Karl Barth, Rudolph Bultmann, and Martin Buber. We read them all, or tried to, but very few of us assimilated what we read in any systematic way. We remembered enough to write papers and pass exams, but very few of us going on for ordination and parish ministry found in theology as a systematic study anything which gripped us or changed how we looked at God and the world. What we did find were bits and pieces of theology here and there. Our minds, for the most part, were too shaped by our pre-seminary education to grasp the grand metaphorical themes of Barth and Niebuhr, or the dense philosophical abstractions of Tillich. Certain doctrines affected us more than others, particularly doctrines of sin. Seminarians seemed to join schools of degrees of fallenness. Some already taken with existentialism went to the Neo-Orthodox low doctrine of human nature, while others, more influenced by Clinical Pastoral Education or a previous infatuation with Freud, were more inclined to accept Tillich's concept of alienation. Cheerful types somehow wrested from Buber a more hopeful assessment of human potential. But generally speaking those of us seeking the parish ministry—rather than graduate school and a doctorate—found more meaning in C.P.E. and pop pastoral theologians like Reuel Howe, who mixed Buber and Tillich and the insights of psychotherapy into a respectable whole which seminarians could respond to and assimilate and, more important for a parish minister, communicate.

Looking back on it, there were three doctrines of the church that were distorted in seminary even by the early fifties.

The first is the doctrine of salvation. Somehow, with much biblical exegesis and reference to pastoral psychology, salvation was trivialized; it began to be equated with the health and wholeness and healing of individuals. This fitted the whole business into pastoral counseling and did away with any need for a transcendent God who saves. We had no way of thinking about a transcendent God who saves even though many of us had been encountered by a transcendent God who saved us. There was little room for religious experience as theology was taught in the main line seminaries at that time.

The second doctrine which we found difficult to understand and assimilate, perhaps because salvation had been trivialized, was justification through grace by faith. We heard a great deal about it and discussed earnestly among ourselves the argument between faith and works, but whatever we professed, we believed in works.

A third theological misapprehension many seminarians picked up was their understanding of Niebuhr's doctrine of sin, a doctrine which required a powerful doctrine of salvation not sufficiently emphasized in seminary. As we understood it, original sin was so powerful a force in the human aggregate of a nation that nations could not be expected to act in a moral manner. The best that could be expected of nation-states was a balance of power among them sufficient to make aggression on the part of one nation too costly to pursue. But this doctrine of sin, dubious as it was at the level of relations between nations, and later regretted by Niebuhr as he saw it used to justify the Vietnam War, was just as regrettably used by too many ministers to justify hardball fundraising methods, or various forms of power politics in church affairs. It has become increasingly obvious that a heavy doctrine of sin can and should not be used as an excuse for sinning.

Seminary exposure to theology, then, was for many of us superficial; to a degree it was even spiritually damaging. We acquired an overlay of theological material which we could recite on demand, seizing bits and pieces of theology eclectically, here and there, which fit into our customarily empirical and psychotherapeutic way of thinking.

Where we found the depth in our seminary training was in the study of Scripture. Again, our methods were empirical, and it is too bad that we were never taught to go beyond historical criticism in our approach to the Bible. Stripping the Bible to the bare bones of its revelation was a fascinating task, and in the end a profoundly theological task, but no one knew what to do with the God that it revealed. We had no language, no paradigm, to help us articulate what we found. The God discovered in narrative does not translate into descriptive language, cannot be set as a problem to be solved, as Northrop Frye has so eloquently proved. We were, then, aware that the God of Scripture was both preposterous in empirical terms, which were all we had to think with, and yet powerfully attractive precisely because this God called those very terms into question.

If we learned nothing else from Scripture, we learned that there was something utterly other than the world we lived in, as defined by its own terms, which beckoned to us even though our terms were the terms of the world. We didn't know it at the time, but this inarticulate, not-quite-understood relationship to the world of Scripture and to reality defined in narrative scriptural terms, was faith. We

trusted something which we could not set as a problem
and solve, something we could not put to the uses of our
ambition because we couldn't appropriate it and make it
ours. We could only be addressed by it and perhaps, at
the very least, be to some degree shaped by it as, to the
best of our ability, we struggled to respond.

Thus it was with a poorly assimilated mixture of
theology and psychotherapeutic theory that many of us
had our formation in seminary during the fifties and early
sixties. We were far more inclined to use therapeutic
theory than theology as a basis for judgment and decision
where we saw any conflict between the two. Many of us
came to seminary as young veterans of World War Two,
much concerned about Christianity as it related directly to
our existence. In a sense we had used seminary as a place
to reflect on and make sense out of our war experience.
Our appearance in seminary coincided with the rise of
Clinical Pastoral Education, and C.P.E. in its earliest
incarnation was largely based in mental hospitals. There
the young veterans were thrown in with young
psychiatric residents, often lectured to by teaching
psychiatrists, and generally exposed to a great deal of
what was at first Freudian, but later became more eclectic
psychiatric theory.

For many of us, C.P.E. was the most exciting and
shaping experience we had in our seminary education.
The courses we took in seminary were for the most part
compulsory and dryly academic; no one suggested to us
that in the whole there might be something that would
make sense out of our individual and corporate life.
C.P.E., on the other hand, taught people who had been
numbed and hardened by their war experience to feel
again, let them test themselves in complex and frightening

situations and then provided a place and a theoretical base for reflecting on their response. From the C.P.E. experience came a demand on the part of seminarians for counseling courses, and soon pastoral theology became almost synonymous with counseling. For lay Christians as well as for people outside the church completely, the minister became the person you went to when you were "troubled."

The role of pastoral counselor was generally blessed by a society which needed it, and there were many sociological, demographic reasons for its sudden popularity. After the war the American middle class suddenly became transient, either moving deftly by their own choice to where the money was, or being moved by their corporations whether they liked it or not. All upward mobility in the corporations depended on a willingness to move laterally.

This was hard enough for the men, but for the women, for many, many women, it was impossible to do with three kids under five and still remain sane. Except in the metropolitan centers, psychiatrists were absent or in short supply—largely because if they set up practice in the suburbs, they starved. It could hurt you socially or professionally if it became known that you were seeing a psychiatrist. Men tended to feel the same way about ministers, but women had to see *someone* and their husbands didn't feel humiliated, or *as* humiliated, if they saw a minister for counseling.

Thus one function of pastoral counseling in the fifties and sixties—and I suspect still, to a lesser degree—was to supply the only source of professional support for women victimized by the management practices of the great corporations. The trouble was that too few of the pastor-counselors understood that the depression of their client-parishioners was not the result of neurosis, but a normal reaction to constantly being moved from one anonymous suburb to another and having to add to their loss of friends and a familiar environment the endless demands of uprooted children and a depressed husband.

Less perceptive pastor-counselors accepted the women's own diagnosis of themselves as in some way sick or neurotic; they could hardly do more than compensate for what the harsh diagnosis did to the self-esteem of these women by providing them with a place to ventilate.

Another function of counseling for the parish minister was simply to be the only available professional person to deal with people who were mentally ill. The absence of psychiatrists and trained social workers in rural and suburban areas left only the parish minister. If he had done his C.P.E. in a mental hospital he could identify true psychosis and help with a committal, or, for lack of someone better trained, he could provide whatever therapy he was capable of, advise the family, be of some help. Ministers who did their C.P.E. in mental hospitals were trained in group therapy, learning to identify and deal with individual maladaptive behavior as it is revealed in group interactions, rather than sensitivity training. Most parish ministers later had training in group process, but their earlier training in group therapy often subtly, or not too subtly, influenced their group theory and technique.

Probably the most valuable thing which the therapeutic model provided for the parish minister was a new sensitivity to loss. The parish minister was the traditional person in the community to deal with death. Death and dying and the assault on meaning that accompanies them have always been at the center of the vocation of the ordained minister, yet as the education and values of Western culture became more and more empirical, the traditional mode of ministering to the dying or to survivors, the classic mode of consolation, became less and less helpful. Ministers knew this better than anyone else, and were among the first people to see the importance of the new warning from psychiatrists that grief must be taken seriously and worked with.

In the early days, certainly up to the early sixties, there was a lot of resistance to the trend toward therapeutic language and assumptions. For one thing, parish clergy would often talk psycho-babble or even preach it — their reference to psychiatric or counseling jargon was constant. Where they had a degree of charisma, they would build up constituencies in the parish who spoke their language. The pastor's allies often referred to others in the parish suspicious of the therapeutic world-view as "rigid," or "square," or "uptight," or even "sick." Ministers were attacked for being nothing but social workers or two-bit shrinks, but since the attacks often came from conservatives — if not political reactionaries — in the parish, we tended to ignore those attacks and explain them away as a form of neurotic aberration. The critics, we said, had authority problems, or suffered from rigidity of personality. It is my guess that a fair number of these critics withdrew from those parishes where the therapeutic model reigned, in order to go to other more traditional parishes, or else left the church altogether.

At any rate the therapeutic model seemed to triumph briefly as counseling and group work became the most important nonliturgical part of a parish minister's vocation. Civil rights, the war in Vietnam, radical changes in the role of women, economic insecurity, an unstable economy, and many other things besides reduced the amount of counseling and group work for the minister, but the language and values of therapy had become assimilated into the mainline middle-class white churches.

I should point out here that the therapeutic model had from the beginning been a white middle-class phenomenon. In this sense it was very exclusive, and where white middle-class ministers tried to counsel black parishioners, middle-class or otherwise, they often did more harm than good. Where they tried to counsel white working class people they usually got nowhere.

Today pastoral counseling has become largely a specialty. Counseling specialists have an M.Div. and are usually ordained, often with an advanced degree in clinical psychology as well; they work in clinics, particularly those sponsored by local churches, or serve on the staff of wealthy parishes, or just go into private practice. The difference between them and other therapists is not always clear, and there is no consensus on how they should relate biblical or theological material to counseling.

Huge numbers of people also call themselves "therapists." Many of them are unmonitored and uncredentialed, yet so far many states have decided to let them alone because the number of people demanding therapy is so much greater than credentialed therapists could handle, and because most therapists, however eccentric, have a passionate constituency that would not take kindly to seeing its therapist prosecuted. The therapist and his or her constituency can be like a religious cult; indeed, the state's attitude towards "therapy" seems to resemble its attitude towards the church.

The parish minister today, then, is surrounded by pastoral counselors, therapists of many stripes, psychiatrists, clinical psychologists, social workers, and even an occcasional psychoanalyst. It is no longer difficult to make a referral, though it may be risky. Moreover, the time that parish clergy once gave to counseling has on a somewhat limited scale been more often assigned to spiritual direction; the image of the parish minister as "pastor to the troubled" has, in white middle-class America, been supplanted by the parish minister as a low-profile crisis manager. The management paradigm is taking over the therapist paradigm. Spiritual direction may, for some ministers, be a means of giving their managerial image the odor of sanctity. For others, if we can believe priests with decades of experience in spiritual direction, it is too often a matter of giving *counseling* the odor of sanctity, which is not what it is intended for.

So much for my sketch of the history of pastoral counseling, however brief and inadequate. It should not be inferred from this history that the pastor-counselor was the sole cause of the therapeutic culture becoming the moral context of the parish. The same thing was happening to the culture of management, to public education, to art, to television. All were pervaded with therapeutic metaphors and values. The culture of the parish would have been deeply affected even if ministers had radically opposed therapeutic values from the start, as a fair number did.

What happened to the role of the parish priest in all of this? Where the priest began to be perceived, and in some cases perceived himself, as a counselor for troubled people, the personality of the priest suddenly became more important to the church than his calling. The traditional doctrine of priesthood, the doctrine of the priest as mediator between the congregation and God, was lost when the priest as "caring person" seemed to take on the very role of God. The warm, open, nonjudgmental, compassionate human being, free of the rigidities of the priestly role, putting aside the distancing of the traditional pastor, took the suffering of his parishioners upon himself. Whether he engaged in classical long-term counseling or not, the values of counseling became part of his leadership style. Don Browning points out that this included the "bracketing of morality," that is, putting morality aside in the counseling process, assuming it was still the guiding principle of the parish, on the grounds that it was perhaps too much a part of the client's burdensome conscience. No blame!

Beginning in the fifties bishops also began to look as closely at psychiatric screening reports and C.P.E. evaluations as they did at any other data about their candidates for ordination.

Yet it was also at this point that therapeutic and priestly roles began to jar on one another. First the civil rights movement and then the Vietnam War took on an ethical importance the church could not ignore. However when the parish priest rose to the pulpit to preach against the evils of racism or the Vietnam War, the congregation became confused. "He was never judgmental before. He was so warm and open. He cared so much for our potential as human beings, and here he is telling us that we are sinful and responsible for the suffering of millions. He has betrayed us. Let us crucify him!" And in many cases they did, saying, "He said we should care about one another, but he didn't care about us."

This same period was the period of the great divorce. Wave after wave of divorces swept over the congregations—and by the end of the sixties, over the clergy like everybody else. Those sitting in our congregations today in their thirties and early forties are the children of those divorces. Half of them were, as they perceived it, abandoned by one parent, who was almost always the father. So what can clergy expect if they let themselves be "in loco parentis"? Particularly if we insist on being called "Father"?

The management style toward which clergy have recently been shifting is an attempt to avoid these consequences of symbolic parenthood. "I'm not your parent. I refuse to infantilize you. I will not put up with your pathological dependency. (Echoes of the therapeutic model). I am a kindly professional here to facilitate *your* ministry to one another or to the community. You must set your own goals and I will help you achieve them. You must help one another develop your full potential in a pluralistic community, respecting each other's gifts (or space). The key is mutual ministry" (or shared ministry. There is vast confusion about which is which).

Clergy have moved from the warm, open, non-judgmental parent model, which was basically therapeutic, to what was too often perceived as the angry blaming parent model, based on social ethics but often lacking theological grounding, to the management model. The latter is practical; it addresses the catastrophic potential in playing God, or rather, in being everyone's parent without bringing God into it much at all. Yet the trouble with clergy functioning as managers and professionals is that it still makes impossible demands upon the parish priest's personality.

I suppose the most often-read book on this subject is John Harris' *Stress, Power, and Ministry*. I assign it every year in my Parish Ministry course at E.D.S, where the reaction of seminarians is interesting. One told me, "I hope Harris is wrong about all of a parish priest's power lying in his or her authenticity. The kind of authenticity he describes would take four years of analysis to accomplish, if you were lucky." Another comments, "After reading *Stress, Power, and Ministry* I have lost any desire I might have had to be a parish minister. I don't want any job where I have to spend so much time getting people's approval of me as a person before I can begin to do with assurance the things my job requires me to do. If there is no authority in priesthood itself, not even the authority of one agreed-upon purpose for it, who needs it?" Yet Harris honestly tries to come to grips with the theological significance and purpose of ordination; unfortunately, it is a weak and unconvincing part of the book compared to Harris' emphasis on personal authenticity—a therapeutic criterion if ever there was one.

Far more revealing and disturbing than *Stress, Power, and Ministry* is a pamphlet I saw recently issued by the Council for the Development of Ministry in the Episcopal Church. It was entitled *Healthy Relationships Between Priests and People: Diocesan and Congregational Soundings*, by Florence Ross. The word "healthy" in the title is not merely the random use of a therapeutic word to catch our attention. As it turns out, health and sickness are the only two criteria by which relationships between priest and people are evaluated. And guess who's sick? Guess who has the ulcer?

Fifteen diocesan bishops, a handful of church consultants and a very few lay persons from fewer parishes see the sickness in rigid, authoritarian priests, burned-out priests, priests unequipped by continuing education with skills to manage conflict, priests who are not warm and caring. There is hardly any quarrel with the sickness-health metaphor except from Florence Ross, the consultant cursed with having to make sense out of this flood of conflicting information.

Health and sickness, she explains again and again, are subjective criteria from which only impressionistic evaluations can be drawn. No mention is made of the actual issues from which conflicts spring, no consensus reached on a doctrine of priesthood, not even a job description for the parish minister emerges. Consultants tend to see all health in the priest-congregation relationship in terms of surgical intervention, a radical fix, a new set of management techniques. There are flashes of light, solitary insights of a bishop here, a consultant there, but the overall impression of this discussion of priest and congregation is not just one of confusion, but of angry disagreement and conflict as well. Disagreement and conflict as to the etiology, diagnosis and treatment of a disease. The pamphlet reveals the extent to which the church is part of the therapeutic culture, and we should make no mistake, the management model is as pervaded by therapeutic theory as any other.

But so am I. For years I have tended to think and act within the parameters of therapeutic theory and I am still convinced that many therapeutic insights are not only useful to the parish priest, but consonant with the gospel of Jesus Christ. What I am taking to task here is the unexamined assumptions of therapeutic theory that have been assimilated as world view, which by its pragmatism and reductionism is often in radical conflict with Christianity. The basis of the conflict lies in therapy's scientific, or at least scientistic, idea that human suffering and conflict can be set as a problem and solved, that suffering is a disease to be cured and an illness from which humans can be healed—healed in empirical terms.

Christianity is a terrible problem solver. It is not a spiritual technology nor a social or psychological technique; it runs into little but frustration and despair whenever it sees itself in this light. Freud was not confused on this issue. His view of life was profoundly tragic. He claimed nothing more for psychoanalysis than an increased ability to deal with the normal suffering of the human condition, honestly faced. The purpose of religion—and not merely Christianity—is to help human beings to find meaning and purpose in life, given inevitable suffering and conflict and assuming that the ultimate threat to meaning is the given that we must die.

The ultimate insanity of viewing life as a problem to be solved can be seen in the Holocaust. Hitler referred to it as the final solution to the Jewish problem. He justified it on the basis of genetic engineering: it would clear up the human gene pool. We are now faced with the final solution to the human problem, or perhaps even the problem of life itself with all its suffering: nuclear war. Even psychiatry is beginning to look towards genetic engineering, the purely biological realm from which it emerged and where "maladaptive" behavior can be understood in hard, quantified, measurable terms and fixed, solved.

Christianity deals with suffering in a totally different way. For St. Paul, as William Stringfellow interpreted him, to sin was to accept the notion that death made all suffering meaningless, and to behave in a way that would provide as much pleasure as possible and assure survival as long as possible. This, for Paul, was to live under the rule of sin and death, the rule of Satan. It makes every individual the adversary of every other; self-concern becomes the primary motivation of human existence. Sounds like a description of the American way of life, doesn't it?

Christianity insists that the true and only God took on the human condition with all its suffering, including death itself, and through sacrifical love redeemed it, made it meaningful, holy and good. By so doing, God in Christ overcame the rule of death, the rule of Satan, and made human community possible on a different level than that of corporate survival. Survival as a corporate or individual goal is, for human beings, the most illusory goal of all. We don't survive. But with God's help we can overcome the fear of death through sacrificial love, through trust that death does not have the ultimate word about the human condition, through faith in the resurrection from the dead. Our freedom lies with God's help in choosing the suffering which goes with sacrificial love, rather than enduring the inevitable random suffering of biological existence, try as we might to find pleasure and assure our own survival.

The therapeutic world-view, empirical and scientific, can make no sense out of Christianity. For biology there is no other purpose for life than the survival of the genes. A chicken is an egg's way of making another egg. An adaptive chicken is a big one that triumphs in the pecking order and gets to lay more eggs.

Sacrifice? Deliberately taking on the pain of self-diminishment for the sake of another? You mean masochism, you mean a real problem with self-esteem — unless of course it has a realistic short-term payoff.

Symbiosis? Sure. But sacrifice? Let's face reality, winning is not the most important thing, winning is the *only* thing. We're talking the survival of the fittest.

Love? Well, of course. Everyone needs love, a complementary partner who understands and accepts us for who we are to support us in the rat race. Can't survive without it. But face it, love is not for ever. Keep your options open. The mature person knows when he or she has outgrown a partner.

Community? Sure, everyone needs a group of supportive peers who share one's interests. But pick your friends carefully. They can do you a world of good, but a bad choice can really mess you up.

And so it goes. The therapeutic world view gnaws at our Christianity at the same time that the failure of a consensus about what priesthood is makes it more and more difficult for us to lead a parish. This is becoming readily and painfully apparent, as the following example will show. There is a comparatively new phenomenon in the relationship of priest and parish, the involuntary termination—that is, firing—of clergy by their parishioners. Compare the way a diocesan consultant, say, and a parish priest would look at this. The diocesan consultant will probably identify the "symptoms" of this disease as clergy burn-out, alcohol abuse, divorce, and irreconcilable conflict with the congregation. The priest will pin the blame on an oversupply of clergy for parish vacancies, decreased clergy mobility—"getting stuck"—and higher expectations of the clergy on the part of the laity. The consultant's assessment will be therapeutic, the priest's structural, demographic, and managerial.

Isn't there another way to look at this? Currently, church thinking about the therapeutic society seems to lead in two different directions. One group believes that pastoral counseling and its essentially Freudian assumptions are and always have been evil—breeders of immorality, determinism, and despair. Such people believe that some sort of literalist or fundamentalist Christianity should be put in their place. Another, more academic group seems to hold that all this inward-looking, apolitical individuation is a bourgeois plot to adjust wayward members of the middle class to a basically self-concerned entrepreneurial model, and wish to substitute a brand of activist liberation theology—as Marxist as it is Christian.

So there are two alternatives to the therapeutic and management models. Both claim biblical and theological warrant, yet since each tends to be so adversarial, neither seems adequately Christian. The chapters to follow search for some other direction or some modification of these models. It is not an easy thing to do, for it involves getting some sort of handle on cultural change, an enormously complex process.

My own theory is that culture derives from whatever shared assumptions a society has about how the world works as the result of its being one way rather than another. A coherent culture assumes a single reality; in the long run, all perceptions of that reality will be judged on its own terms. At the heart of cultural change is paradigm shift, a kind of corporate metanoia. It arises from a society's growing consensus that a new way of understanding the world is closer to that world's reality, and closer to the truth. The new paradigm can be quite wrong. Yet it can also be corrected, sometimes by catastrophe, but more often by an accumulation of discrete first-order changes that seep up into society's grand world view and begin to call it into question by throwing everything into turbulence and conflict.

At the deepest level, what Americans seem to believe makes the world work is evolutionary biology. Not evolutionary biology in all its contemporary complexity and sophistication, but evolutionary biology in its crudest, most reductionist form: the survival of the fittest individual carrying the fittest genes. We put what hope we have in natural selection.

What is most wrong with counseling theory or therapeutic insight is its assimilation into a culture shaped by this crude Social Darwinist paradigm. At the heart of this paradigm lies the belief that all relationships are basically adversarial. Consequently, "healthy" insights gained in therapy are those that give us the competitive edge; the greatest benefit of therapy itself is the overall improvement in one's ability to be assertive, to compete, to get over neurotic passivity and self-doubt and become effectively aggressive. In other words, insights about one's own psyche can be used to understand the vulnerabilities of others, and to use them to one's own advantage. Psychiatric theory is a veritable gold mine for the power-hungry and the manipulative, who regard winning as a metaphor for survival, scared people who in their own minds are scratching out a bare existence.

For ministers fighting to survive in a parish, therapeutic theory can become an effective weapon for use in fund drives, in preaching, in adult education, in vestry meetings, in order to get what they want. Indeed therapeutic theory is for some ministers hardly more than a sophisticated set of street smarts; for others, no more than an elaborate language for blaming their congregations and justifying themselves.

Yet for still other pastors, a judicious and theologically selective use of therapeutic theory can be helpful. It can be valuable in preparing a kind of interim community, where a nostaligic moralism does not make morality irrelevant in crucial areas of human life, and parishioners may still see the moral dimension of the decisions and commitments that they actually make. The importance of counseling theory for a serious Christian lies in the way certain of its insights can contribute to the reduction of distrust, lowering the level of shared paranoia and building a spirited environment in which to worship God. It can help to build a moral community, a community with agreed-upon guidelines for a humane corporate life.

In the following chapters I shall look first at two insights of therapeutic theory that are of great value in the practice of parish ministry, and which have at least symbolic confirmation in the New Testament: the phenomenon of transference and countertransference, and the dynamics of loss and change. I shall pay special attention to the cultural significance of these insights.

Then I shall examine three functions of parish ministry — preaching, administration, and liturgy — to see how they have been changed by therapeutic theory, and the extent to which this change has theological or scriptural warrant. Last, I shall discuss the parish as a moral world: its history, its current dynamics, and its possibilities for the future.

The Hedgehog and the Fox

One of the more common experiences of parish ministers often occurs when, with all necessary work for the day finished, and supper eaten and the dishes washed, they sit reading a book. There is a knock at the door, and the minister reluctantly puts aside the book, goes to the door, and opens it to find a somewhat disheveled man, perhaps in early middle age, unshaven, smelling slightly of alcohol, who says that he is broke and out of a job and needs thirty dollars for a bus ticket to Albany where his family is. He assures the minister that he can quickly mail back the thirty dollars if he can just get to Albany. This may be the fourth such supplicant of this kind to knock on the minister's door in a month, or, in the city, in a week.

It is important to ask, "Why the minister?" On a superficial level one can say because ministers are an easy touch, and most alcoholics have learned in the long, slow descent of their alcoholism that this is the case. In point of fact most ministers know enough about alcoholism never to give thirty dollars to an unknown alcoholic, and I shall discuss this below, but alcoholics continue to knock on the doors of parsonages even though they know that their chances of a score are slight. The thing is more of a ritual than a transaction.

But there is somewhere in the dazed consciousness of the alcoholic a kind of belief that ministers ought to "help" him. That's their trade. As Voltaire said of God, "He will forgive me. That's his business." The alcoholic, rapidly sobering, broke, without shelter, on the edge of the "horrors," is looking for some lost parent, some parental person, who will rescue him, or, just as likely, some lost parent who will say, "No. Go away!", thereby reaffirming the alcoholic's view of the cosmos as uncaring, and justifying his alcoholism even more. "These ministers are all alike. They preach love, but when the chips are down they're like everyone else (like my parents). They cop out." Some alcoholics knock on the door to be rescued, some to be rejected. In neither case are their expectations rational or realistic. I have been regaled by alcoholics with stories of the hypocrisy and hard-heartedness of ministers, and I have heard alcoholics state with passion that the only people in the world you can turn to when you're down and out are priests (or ministers.)

What the minister is dealing with here is a kind of ready-made, hardened transference. The alcoholic, even before the door opens, has transferred on to the minister the expectations of authority shaped by his experience of parents and parent figures during his early childhood.

But this is not what the minister is dealing with. Most parish ministers deal with alcoholics at the door in the same fashion. They send them away without giving them any money, saying, "If you want to sober up, come back here tomorrow morning sober and we'll talk about your going to A.A." They know that the alcoholic won't show up, but they hope that the reference to A.A., added to other such references to A.A. from other rejecting ministers, will ring a bell when the alcoholic bottoms out and is really looking for help. They obey the counseling theory dictum, "Never reinforce passive dependent behavior. Don't try to counsel or help an alcoholic in any way when he or she is not sober."

But one parish minister may have very different feelings from another in his or her encounter with an alcoholic. One may be disgusted and angry at him and barely able to keep the disapproval out of her voice. Another may suffer considerable guilt at having to reject him, and has to exert considerable will power not to ask him in to feed him and try to sober him up, and offer him a bed. Another can't handle the guilt and slips him five dollars while sending him away. Another forgets counseling theory, puts on her coat and drives him to a shelter for a night. Another asks him in, calls the bus station and asks the price of a ticket to Albany, finds out it's twenty dollars, confronts him angrily and shows him the door.

Most ministers follow the counseling theory procedure of rejection, mentioning A.A. with the opportunity for help left open. Most do it with a degree of emotional pain, but the pain of each can come from quite different causes. The pain the minister is going through, which may or may not determine the ultimate response, is countertransference.

The rational and probably the most loving course is usually the one followed. The resistance that has to be overcome to follow it is the countertransference, or at least a part of it. Without the countertransference, either positive or negative, there would be no motivation at all, just "Get lost, sucker!" and back to the novel. But the distaste of a minister who was once an alcoholic's child or sister or brother may, ironically, through guilt, incline the minister to do too much or go too far, whereas the deeply-felt compassion of a minister whose childhood was rich with rescue fantasies might find it easier to do less, because she is free to see that less really is better and more loving.

So much for a reductionist version of some of the complexity of countertransference. In simpler and more useful terms, it occurs when people begin to behave toward you as a person with power, wisdom, expertise and superior status, and your emotional response towards those people can range anywhere from passionate love to violent hatred. Even when it is a relatively mild feeling, such a response is usually inappropriate to your relationship with those people. Wherever these feelings come from, they will affect your behavior whenever you are *in loco parentis* if you don't learn to deal with them one way or another.

Perhaps the best place to learn about the fine points of transference-countertransference is in Janet Malcolm's book, *Psychoanalysis, the Impossible Profession*. Her description of this most basic dynamic of the counseling or therapeutic relationship is especially clear because it is presented historically. Janet Malcolm doesn't just tell us what transference-countertransference is, she tells the story of how Freud discovered it and that helps us to discover in our own experience the same phenomenon. She makes it authentic for us in a way that an abstract description never can. I make this observation early on because the therapeutic culture tends to be ahistorical, to neglect the larger historical matrix. Looking at things historically is one alternative to looking at things therapeutically.

I make transference-countertransference into one word to begin with because I want to emphasize the dynamics in the play between the two. Everyone is caught in this play at some point in their lives. Anyone who has ever had (as they used to say) a crush on a teacher, anyone who has ever said of the surgeon before an operation, "It's amazing what a warm, caring, sensitive person Dr. Smith *is*, considering that she is probably the greatest oncologist practicing in the United States today," anyone who has ever worshipped his coach, or hung on every word of her professor, or hyperventilated when arrested for speeding, or suffered anxiety when called in to a conference with one's child's teacher. Anyone who has experienced any of these things has experienced transference. When faced with a person who is more or less *in loco parentis*, acting symbolically in a parent's role, we regress and transfer onto this parent-figure a positive or negative childhood experience.

Transference doesn't even require that one person in the relationship actually be *in loco parentis*. In marriage or friendship, particularly under stress, one person may regress and make child-like demands on the other, pleading in some direct or devious way to be parented. In strong friendships and marriages both partners are willing to take on a parent's role when required, and both dare to regress and be dependent.

Janet Malcolm quotes some very useful material from a paper by an analyst named Leo Stone about something he calls "the primary transference" or "the primordial transference." This, Stone hypothesizes, "derives from [a] craving for the omnipotent parent of early infancy. This craving is universal and can be activated by doctors, politicians, clergy, and teachers as well as analysts."

Malcolm also says that the idea of transference is the only concept of Freud's that has never been questioned within the psychoanalytic community. It is the central dynamic of the therapeutic relationship. What the patient transfers onto the analyst, as it is revealed in words and behavior, is the data of the patient's inner life; it must be interpreted by the analyst back to the patient. It is the heart of the psychoanalytic process.

I think it safe to say that it is the heart of all counseling or therapeutic theory as well, although it may be used in quite different ways. In Neuro-Linguistic Programming, a system of therapy aimed entirely at the elimination of symptoms and which seems to go about its business like a mechanic fixing a truck, the therapist asks the patient to describe the symptoms, watches the patient's eyes, and does a spot check on grammatical constructions, checking out cognitive peculiarities. Then the therapist tells the patient to *do* something, like "Go to Filene's Basement at 9:30 on Saturday morning and faint!"

Now the therapy depends on two things, the patient doing what he is told and, more important, trusting the counselor enough to do it, however outlandish. This last depends on an instant positive transference. Corporation executives are paying large sums per session for this kind of therapy. Would you give large sums up front to a therapist to cure some painful neurotic symptom without first being convinced that she was the Messiah at least?

One can even get a transference on a machine. Joseph Weizenbaum, a world-famous computer scientist at M.I.T., programmed a computer to respond as a Rogerian counselor. He did it to test some of the limits of programming; he had no interest in counseling per se. The program was called Eliza, after the heroine of Shaw's play *Pygmalion.* Weizenbaum published a paper about it in a scientific journal and began to get letters from psychiatrists all over the country who wanted to try it out in mental hospitals so that they could "process" many more patients a day. Weizenbaum was appalled and did all he could to discourage such use of his program.

I submit that this is a serious and unexamined matter. What is the extent of the transference that can take place between a television set and its owner? Why was Ronald Reagan elected president?

At the heart of transference itself lie the issues of trust and safety, very touchy issues in our society. A computer is trustworthy; it won't turn on you. It is predictable. It is user-friendly and will not scold or ridicule you for your mistakes, or punish you if you erase. You can trust its confidentiality, too. But most of all a computer creates the illusion that *you* control *it* completely. There is nothing to fear. You are safe.

Casper Weinberger once said on television, and I heard him say it from the bottom of his heart, that Star Wars was the only hope we have. It is his assurance that we can build a huge, fail-safe electronic dome over our country that protects us from the evil empire which gives Mr. Weinberger hope. This is the political dimension of transference. The person who can charismatically promise safety and cultivate trust has enormous political power, even if the promises are not altogether plausible.

Star Wars, a computer, both are trustworthy. You can be safe with them, trust them in a way you can never trust human beings. The same is true of the Mercedes Benz, or the CAT scan, or perhaps soon, the artificial heart. Soon genetic research and eventually genetic engineering will begin to make human beings more predictable and hence trustworthy and safe to be with, or even safe to be.

There seems to be a kind of hidden consensus in America that we live in a humanly untrustworthy world, where no one is safe. I think of reading an article in "Commentary" that contained the following sentence: "For those so naive as not to understand that all human relationships are basically adversary relationships, this may come as a surprise." In the same vein, several years ago I spent some time looking for a place to live in Cambridge, Massachusetts. It turned out that the real estate companies had zoned Cambridge according to crime rate and charged higher rents and sales prices for the safer areas. The endless expensive legal hassle of purchasing a small condo is designed to protect the buyer, the seller, the real estate agent, and the bank all from one another. Each one of the four is the others' adversary.

All this is simply to make the point that in a time of runaway competition, economic turbulence and unsettling social change, transference takes on socio-political dimensions that go far beyond the counseling or therapeutic relationship. People growing up and living in a vaguely menacing and untrustworthy environment tend to make rapid positive or negative transferences towards people who seem trustworthy and promise safety. The tendency is to see all leadership either as phoney and untrustworthy or else as the bearer of salvation.

Countertransference is all the stuff from our early childhood that we bring to a situation where we are in a role of leading, helping, teaching, healing, warning, enforcing, encountering, rescuing, judging, legislating, or consulting. It is all the emotional baggage from our early childhood that we bring to a relationship in which we have actual or symbolic power, in which we are the ones upon whom others depend for something they believe they need and we have.

A particularly dramatic example of countertransference can be seen in the case of a lawyer who turned himself in to the police after hiding out for twenty years. He had had a Black Panther for a client in the sixties who was charged with armed robbery and murder; convinced that his client had been framed, the lawyer had smuggled him in a pistol. The young client tried to force his way out and was killed after shooting several guards. The lawyer's feelings, wherever they came from, had completely overridden his professional judgment. Yet that same countertransference, had he known how to deal with it, would have made him a formidable legal advocate for his client.

The issue that concerns me here is how the transference—countertransference phenomenon affects the parish priest. How can the priest or minister deal with it in such a way as to make it an agent of justice and love, rather than simply succumbing to it as a demonic force? For the concept assumes a powerful irrational force in all human interaction. It assumes that people often, perhaps always, are to some degree unaware of *why* they think and do what they think and do. The concept assumes that people are driven by emotion and instinct, rather than drawn forward by purpose, and so leads to what Philip Reiff calls the "hermeneutic of suspicion"—a tendency to attribute motives to others quite different from what they claim their motives to be. It leads to emotive ethics, the theory that all morality or ethics are at any given time a structure of behaviors designed to serve the advantage of those in power. It might also be added that the more sophisticated minister, who has been analyzed and so understands the nuances of transference, can be a manipulative person who uses this sophistication to get and keep power for its own sake.

Perhaps the most disturbing result of the concept of transference-countertransference is a radical reduction of our trust in the freedom of the will. By now it has become a cliche to say that all of the major scientific discoveries since the Renaissance have served to reduce human self-esteem. Galileo removed us from the center of the universe. With his second law of thermodynamics, Newton proved that the power of entropy was supreme, while

Darwin showed us that a human being is an animal like any other, doomed to compete for survival. Freud claimed that the freedom of the will, upon which what remained of our self-esteem was based, was a mere figment of language. Joseph Weizenbaum insists that the computer is making another assault on our self-esteem, displacing people from their jobs and actually regarded by an increasing number of people as more intelligent and useful than they are.

In a culture such as ours, which puts such a high value on freedom, the concept of transference-countertransference with its assumption of major distortions in how we normally "perceive" one another calls into question just how free we are to make rational decisions. How can we respond adaptively to interpersonal situations, or know what we intend to do and why we intend to do it? We see this perhaps most alarmingly in our political process, where the media people who cover it hardly mention the substantive positions of candidates because they assume that these positions are contrived, put together from polling data, with candidates tailored to an image that fits the transferential expectations of the voters. Neither the campaign manager nor the media — nor for that matter the candidate — sees the electoral process as a rational expression of freedom. Even the voters are more inclined to concern themselves with picking a winner than deciding on a president. Identifying with a parent figure who is also a winner, however, seems to make them feel safe, and perhaps "good about themselves."

Yet "good" feelings about oneself are hardly the same as self-respect. People who are regarded by their leaders as regressed and thus deliberately infantilized in the political process often suffer from deep self-contempt.

The issue of self-contempt is a new one. It is not the same as guilt; it has taken the place of pride. In a nuclear world it is of great importance, for the lower our self-esteem, the more likely it seems to us that our enemy might nuke us. Self-esteem is, once again, a therapeutic concept to meet a new large-scale psychic phenomenon. The assumptions about the freedom of the will underlying transference-countertransference are not likely to enhance human self-regard. Indeed, to believe that the most primal, basic human motivation stems from a craving for the safe parental environment of early infancy, is to reduce the human condition to a state of pure biology—if this belief is held in an empirical culture such as ours.

Yet something very like this belief was, for New Testament writers, one powerful metaphor for the sinful human condition. The Epistle to the Hebrews puts it succinctly: "The children of a family share the same flesh and blood. And so Jesus, too, shared ours, so that through death he might break the power of him who had death at his command, that is, the devil; and might liberate those who through fear of death had all their lifetime been in servitude."

According to Hebrews, it is the fear of death that makes us slaves, childish, obedient to anyone (Satan) who promises safety. Politicians, advertisers, evangelical ministers, insurance companies, and the entire T.V. enterprise relentlessly inform us that if we don't accept their guidance and protection, we're dead. Not dead in the literal sense of being a corpse, but metaphorically dead, as academics—"Publish or perish," "Under the 600's on your GRE's and you're dead"—politics—"If he doesn't win in New Hampshire, he's dead meat"— or sports—"The Celtics are staying alive, but if they don't win this one, they're history!" (history understood as a pile of corpses). Dead, in this sense, means loser, out of the competition, and since we must compete to "survive" then certainly as good as dead, or, perhaps, as bad as dead, for death is a very bad thing. Death is for losers.

It is the fear of death which makes us slaves, says the Letter to the Hebrews. Yet in our time we have the fear of death, a kind of survival terror, becoming the primary motivator for American society. This may be the first culture in history which has as its purpose exacerbating rather than mitigating the fear of death. The result is a kind of endemic regression that in turn leaves too many Americans at all times vulnerable to impulsive and irrational positive or negative transference.

Within the therapeutic culture, regressive transference outside of an actual therapeutic relationship is considered pathology. Indeed a major goal of therapy is for the client to become less and less dependent on the therapist. For humanistic psychology, the primary goal of therapy is some sort of individual autonomy for the client (autonomy — literally from the Greek — a law unto oneself).

The concept of individual autonomy may be the craziest idea since the flat world, and for the same reason. By kidding oneself one can get from day to day believing in it, but autonomy has nothing to do with reality. Human beings, simply as a part of nature, are inextricably dependent on each other as well as dependent on the physical world. The anomaly inherent in this concept of autonomy can be discovered in therapy itself, where things may go along in a helpful way until the matter of termination comes up. At this point things have a tendency to go very wrong. Clients quit. Clients regress. Clients make a pass at their therapist. Clients forget the insights they have learned. Very few courses of therapy end in a way that both therapist and client consider good. As a parish minister I found that a fair number of parishioners who came to me for counseling eventually confessed to be "terminating" after three or four years of psychotherapy. Janet Malcolm writes that the only consensus among psychoanalysts about what constitutes a successful analysis is one terminated by the analyst, not the patient.

Seen theologically, transference is like St. Augustine's restlessness of the heart, or the mystics' emptiness deliberately exposed and cultivated, or becoming like a little child (as Jesus urged us to do). It is an existential category, a given of existence. Humans *do* regress under stress or often for no good reason at all. Regressive transference is neither good nor evil, but the direction it takes is a matter not only of theological consequence, but moral consequence as well.

Erik Erikson and most traditional therapists since have given enormous importance to the concept of basic trust, which comes from trustworthy parenting during the first year of life. On a psychological level basic trust seems to mean our ability to refrain from bringing undue anxiety to the course of a human life, so that it is possible to avoid paranoid tendencies or excessive rigidities and to look forward to the future with the expectation that we will be able to cope with what it brings. On this level trust is more a function of emotion than cognition, more the fruit of individual emotional development than of a culture that mitigates the fear of death and assumes a social responsibility for the place of individuals in community. Basic trust as a first and essential stage of emotional development is not the same thing as religious faith. I have heard a spiritual director insist that someone who has not learned basic trust during the first year of life can never learn to pray. If by prayer is meant some deep form of meditation this may be true, but there is a level of trust, of assurance and cosmic support that can hold people together even when they are regressed, anxious to the point of terror, angry and very depressed, or for that matter when they are emotionally flat and carefully defended from any feelings at all.

Metaphorically speaking there is a kind of heavenly connection, a place in the mind beyond the *sturm und drang* of inner turmoil and pain, that is less related to feelings than to mind and soul and God. It is related to body as St. Paul means body, one's unique all-of-a-pieceness, not body as flesh or biochemical event. It is a calm beyond turbulence yet coexistent with turbulence, a reminder of calm, a peripheral awareness of peace in the midst of turbulence, a conviction that peace and safety are, surprisingly, there. One knows that they are there despite all turbulent feelings to the contrary. This heavenly connection, this grace, this spiritedness, is like news from the outside. It does not depend on some proper functioning of our inwardness, or some ideal upbringing, some good luck in the tight circle of our parents and the environment of our infancy.

This religious faith is nourished by Scripture and liturgy, by acting out at regular intervals the narrative of our salvation from sin and death.

It seems to me that where psychology (the natural conditions of one's inwardness) and God's grace meet is in the phenomenon of transference. There the basic trust or mistrust of parents and parent figures, undefended and in the full power of regression, is touched by grace, and changed. As the author of Hebrews said, those who "had all their lifetime been in servitude through the fear of death are liberated by the one who could through death break the power of Satan."

The priest or minister is the figure that a stable society hopes will be its primary—and safest—object of transference. In Western Christian culture, priests are dressed in black with round collars and provided with sexually ambiguous vestments to wear in leading worship. Male priests are traditionally called "Father" while women priests are increasingly referred to as pastor—another parental title, like shepherd. The use of Reverend as a title presumably means that the minister is to be revered. Where ministers didn't wear clericals, they nonetheless used other distancing procedures. One of these was to pray at the drop of a hat, thereby setting themselves aside as persons of prayer or, before the ordination of women, men of prayer. This had a particularly strong effect, since few other men in American society pray publically at all.

There were many other distancing procedures, known to ministers as tricks of the trade but to lay people as behavior expected of a minister. Single ministers were never to date or marry parishioners. Priests and ministers were not to touch parishioners beyond shaking hands, except for children. Priests were not to be called by their first names. Priests and ministers in most denominations totally dominated the liturgy. Worship was their turf. One was to have no close friends in the parish. One's friends were most appropriately other ministers with whom one could be oneself.

All this distancing came out of the wisdom of the culture, which perceived that one human being can only parent several hundred people from a great distance, as well as from the wisdom of the church, which assumed that the proper focus for a Christian's transference is Jesus Christ. The distant priest, although focusing the transference, does not satisfy its craving; rather, the priest symbolizes the God who will touch this craving with love and transform it into a kind of humanly viable trust of life itself, which is Christian love.

The traditional priest or minister danced out a kind of choreography of care, calling without respect to rank or wealth, ministering to the sick or to elderly shut-ins, praying, teaching, preaching, consoling, warning, feeding, noticing, paying attention, hearing confessions, absolving. None of this was to be done well or badly. None of it depended on the personality, the warmth, the charm, the sensitivity, or the skill of the minister. The minister knew, and lay people expected, that a minister's vocation was to make a theological statement by the orderly round of parish tasks. If the minister did it with grace and charm, so much the better. If the minister did it clumsily, angrily, eccentrically, or boorishly, that was too bad, but not terribly important. Everyone sensed that it was a hard thing to do, precisely because of the necessary distancing; it was probably a lonely life in its eccentricity. Indeed, priesthood has been called a vocation to loneliness.

Now anyone can see that from a counseling theory point of view this understanding of parish ministry is appalling, psychonoxious, bad for the priest, bad for the parishioners. Priests will become locked into their public personae, will lose their identity as persons, will be insensitive to interpersonal dynamics, will lose touch with their feelings, will generally turn into zombies.

As for lay persons, they will see through the inauthentic personalities of the priest or minister, will get a distorted idea of the Christian life as a rigid, guilt-ridden obsession with duty and meaningless routine.

And it all turned out to be true. By the late fifties the traditional parish minister was beginning to be seen as a rigid, cold, distanced, punitive father figure, a kind of spiritual cop. The young graduate of C.P.E., on the other hand, came on as a real human being, warm, open, tolerant, sensitive, not defensive, non-judgmental, supportive, and a sophisticated counselor of troubled people. He was welcomed with open arms and he was often devoured by open mouths, eaten up, used up. Transference, and finally countertransference, did him in. The absence of distance made him the focus, the primary focus, of a transference only God can bear. At first the countertransference was very positive: "These are my sheep, my children who love and trust me. I am a success. My parish is flourishing. How God has blessed me and my people." The countertransference provided real energy and real, felt, concern; the new minister did more good in a week than the traditional minister did in a month. But fifteen years later the same minister might be expressing a very negative reaction: "If these passive-aggressive types don't get off my back, then I'm through!" and they didn't get off his back and he was through, fired, as he got divorced, grew his hair to his waist, bought love beads, had an affair with his secretary, balanced amphetamines with marijuana, did, in fact, anything to get fired so that he could blame the rigidity and intolerance of his parish for his need to get away from its impossible demands. That's a caricature of runaway transference-countertransference, of course, but I saw precisely that happen more than once, and less dramatic catastrophes in abundance.

The effect on women priests of the transference-counter-transference phenomenon can't be seen this early in the process, but there are hints of what is to come. The married male priest who hires a woman curate will have a lot of things to work out with his spouse, the curate and the parish. The wife of a male rector has often had an extensive ministry in the parish. The parish may believe that you can get to the rector through her, which gives her a degree of power, or she may be active in certain parish functions, often serving as a leader. As the rector is "father," so his spouse has often been parish mother. When a woman curate appears, the rector's wife's entire function may be transferred to the curate, including the influencing of the rector. The trouble is that being a curate, whether you are a man or a woman, is very like being the rector's wife. Indeed there is often a close and sympathetic relationship betwen a male curate and rector's wife, since each knows what the other is going through. This same sympathy may not be extended to a woman curate with whom the wife feels herself in competition.

We know that women rectors are getting a surprising number of men in counseling. I say surprising because few men have gone to male ministers for counseling.

Recently a surprising thing happened in a midwestern parish, happened for the first time. In an extended ideological conflict betwen a male social-activist rector and a woman curate more committed to the pastoral model, the rector was fired. This had not been the intention of the curate and she resigned. It is nevertheless the first time in the history of the Episcopal Church that a curate effected the firing of a rector.

Which leads me to a conjecture. Over half of those under forty in any parish may be the children of divorce, and most of these may have experienced the divorce as having been abandoned by their fathers. For these young adults, the mother will have been experienced as the faithful and trustworthy one. We don't know how this will affect the ministry of women, but male priests report it is extremely dangerous for it to leak out that a male rector is looking for another parish. He may suddenly be criticized for a hundred different things and even get fired before he is called to a new church. Too much like old dad fooling around.

Five years used to be a respectable amount of time to spend in a parish before accepting another call. Today I hear male rectors say that real trust just begins at five years. The first five years are spent anxiously working to establish that trust. From the asking around I do, I would gather that women rectors are having less trouble with trust issues, perhaps because there is less actual chance of their being called away, but also because of a more positive and unambivalent transference on the part of her congregration.

Until very recently, of course, the pastor did not "look for a job." He waited for a "call." The "call," an unequivocal request for the minister to come as rector to a new parish, came after the pastor had let it be known to his bishop and/or others with some oversight of the church that he was ready. Or it might have come out of the blue. The parenthood that went with a call was a commitment without time, like blood parenthood. A call was like death, not the choice of the pastor, but the choice of God the Holy Spirit moving in the church. Or the pastor decided it wasn't, and he stayed where he was. But at no point was the pastor out job-hunting as he or she is required to do today.

The one hundred and forty-two things wrong with the old method of "clergy deployment" can be discussed elsewhere. Yet its results in terms of clergy and congregation contentment were at least as good as the results of the contemporary competitive dog and pony shows. As far as the matter of transference went, everything began with a commitment on the part of both parties— plus, among Episcopalians at least, a strong and canonically defined tenure for the pastor. The result was an inclination to trust the institution of the call, and wait patiently for the "fit" to sort itself out, particularly since the "fit" itself was more clearly shaped and defined by canon law, tradition and custom. Transferential passions and distortions took place within this formal structure.

In the current atmosphere of conflict and tension between the pastor and the congregation, the pain lies in the transferential or countertransferential relationship, but this issue is not so psychological as it is theological. The transference is real, it is there to be handled, but it cannot be dealt with by the pastor functioning as a therapist or as a business manager. It is not a problem to be solved in some slick empirical way.

As I sit writing this I see a fox hunting in the pasture below me. My first reaction is to be struck dumb by the graceful sensitivity of this perfect animal to its environment, the complexity of its behavioral responses as it trots, sniffs, stalks, bounds, takes its prey, while constantly alert to its own danger. With a great longing I try to share its concentration, try to imagine its mindless genetic focus on its task. It seems, briefly, a terrible thing to be so painfully separated from the creation by my consciousness. How wonderful to be at one with nature, the beautiful, complex, orderly, vital system of which I am so irretrievably a part, yet not a part.

I am not one with nature. My mind shifts to Empedocles, and I return to my pen and paper. "The fox knows many things. The hedgehog knows one big thing." If I look at this ancient metaphor empirically I find it faulty. Neither the fox nor the hedgehog "knows" anything. Their radically different behaviors are simply genetic variations on the "one big thing" of survival. If I learn anything from this metaphor it is simply, oh, so simply, that adaptive behavior is the *only* thing — really all I need to know. The bottom line. The one big thing that nature teaches. And even evolutionary biology is nothing but chemistry and physics. I become a random biochemical event struggling briefly to survive.

Yet this exquisite metaphor of the hedgehog and the fox echoes across so many years of history to disturb my mind. I think of pastors learning more and more things. How to write a resume. How to mount a job search. How to organize a fund drive. How to resolve congregational conflict, or at least to "manage" it, how to "stay alive" in a hostile congregational environment, how to manage stress through prayer. We are becoming foxes — not in the empirical but the metaphorical sense, learning a complex range of adaptive behaviors to defend ourselves against danger as we stay alive. The hedgehog lives in the knowledge of its own God-given safety, a knowledge nature does not give to human beings.

As Christian pastors our primary concern is not with survival, nature's conditional and temporary reward for street smarts, but with salvation, the issue of revelation and something which is communicated on a radically different level than the empirical.

Empirically, the false safety of transference is the only safety we shall ever know. Theologically this safety is not false in its metaphorical expression. It is about something more profound, something one is not inclined to notice in one's existence without revelation, but which, when discerned, turns existence into life.

Transference-countertransference, then, brings the ambiguities of the conflict between theology — or for that matter Christianity, or for that matter religion — and counseling theory into clear focus. The assumption that transference derives from an infinite need to find safety in an omnipotent parent figure and is simply a given of human existence, pervading all relationships, is demeaning. It is reductionist when viewed within an empirical scientific culture. But its religious isomorph, or metaphor, which is sin understood as bondage to the fear of the ultimate power of death as one part of the total theological statement made by Christianity, provides a way through to the worth of human beings in the eye of God. It also provides a kind of guideline for helping people get beyond the priest or minister with their need to adore, worship, revere, and trust with all their hearts.

It would be nice if in some fundamentalist way we could say transference-countertransference is nonsense. It's not in the Bible and I don't believe in it. But as I have pointed out, it *is* in the Bible, and no contemporary parish priest or minister can avoid its dynamic power for good or evil. Understood purely as a psychological given of the human condition it demeans the human condition. Understood theologically, it takes on a different significance altogether.

But as a psychological or theological phenomenon it will be woven into what authority we have as parish priests or ministers and so will affect all our relationships with our parishioners.

Loss and Change

A few years ago a friend of mine went to the hospital for his nightly visit with his ninety-two year old mother, who was terminally ill. When he had been sitting with her for a few minutes he realized that she was rather less than her usual alert and animated self.

"What's the matter, Mother?" he asked. "The damned minister came again today," she replied. Her angry complaint startled him. She had been a devout church-going, Bible-reading Christian all her life.

"Don't you like him?" he asked. "Oh, he's a nice enough young man and I'm sure he means well. But he won't leave me alone. He keeps asking me questions, and he doesn't like what I say. I can't figure out what he expects me to tell him."

My friend, who is a psychiatrist, groaned. "Doesn't think you're ready to die, does he?" he said, smiling. "That's it. That's exactly it. He seems to think there's some right way to die or something. I don't seem to be miserable enough for him. Why can't he just read me some psalms, or a good passage from Saint Paul? Why can't he just *pray*?"

When my friend left his mother that night, after praying with her and blessing her, he drove to the minister's house and went in to see him.

"Look, Jim," he said to the minister. "*Please*. No Kubler-Ross with my mother. She's ninety-two. She has lived a rich, good, devout Christian life. She's ready. Just read psalms or Bible verses or pray with her, okay?"

The minister looked sheepish. "Tell me the truth, Bob. Did she really tell you that I was doing Kubler-Ross?"

"Of course not. She never heard of Kubler-Ross. She was just confused. Believe me. She's beyond all the stages. She is very comfortable with death."

The minister laughed ruefully. "Right." he said. "I don't know what got into me."

The next night when my friend dropped in to see his mother, she was radiant. "Now I have a proper minister. We can do this thing right!" she said.

I tell this story only to point up where the therapeutic and the theological may jar on one another in the minister's normal round of pastoral care. Elizabeth Kubler-Ross's book *On Death and Dying* was a very perceptive and helpful work for the parish minister. In a thoroughly secular culture, where the denial of death makes death a kind of pervasive hidden agenda, Kubler-Ross provided a way of getting past the unreality of elaborate cultural and psychological defense — learned, indoctrinated defense — into the whole issue of mortality, loss and grief.

The impact of the book was startling and unpredictable. The unthinkable and unspeakable suddenly emerged into the light, not merely for pastors, but through extraordinary media coverage for a whole generation of thoughtful people. But the secular, therapeutic culture has its own defenses. It quickly captured and trivialized what could have been and was intended to be an opening into existential seriousness. Suddenly there was "thanatology." Suddenly the whole matter was reduced to technique. Suddenly death and dying was, in a curious way, an "in" thing. I have called on dying friends who were unduly anxious and miserable because they were not making their way through the stages properly, more concerned for their performance than for death itself.

For pastors, Kubler-Ross's book did not come out of the blue. Most of us had been trained in C.P.E. and seminary courses to work with the grief of survivors; the stages of grief we had learned about and worked with in helping our parishioners deal with loss were not much different from the stages Kubler-Ross identified in the dying person. Again, we thought of our "grief work" as a therapeutic intervention, and grief as a sort of symptom of the pathology of loss, something to be treated.

Here again the medical, the therapeutic model, the notion of loss as an illness with symptoms, tended to become a reductionist if useful category we could add to our professional repertoire. Yet if one really thinks about it, isn't it strange that loss, an absolute given of the human condition which no one will escape, is trivialized to the level of a disease? Loss is an existential category, something that cannot be framed as a problem and solved. It is something that must be lived with, and the only issue is whether we learn to live with it in such a way as to avoid having our own lives damaged beyond repair and made meaningless and burdensome by it.

If pastoral care is the construction of a world in which Christian symbols make a kind of common sense, there must be room in this world for loss and the opportunity for loss to be addressed by these symbols, by the metaphorical, theological language of the church. Grief work as grief work is less than helpful in dealing with the long-term damage loss does to human purposefulness and meaningfulness, critically important though it is in the short run.

What we know about loss as a universal psychological phenomenon comes mainly from two studies, one in London and one in Boston, which took place almost simultaneously. The first is Bowlby's famous study of the effect of taking children from their parents in wartime London for safe keeping in the country. The other, less famous, was directed by a Boston psychiatrist named Eric Lindemann. Lindemann's study began as a result of a major catastrophe, a fire which took place at the Coconut Grove night club in Boston and killed over five hundred young men and women, many of whom were college students. This was in 1942.

Soon after the disaster a number of people began seeking psychiatric help in the Boston area, completely debilitated by grief related to the fire. Parents, siblings, friends, lovers, all needed psychotherapy or even hospitalization. Eric Lindemann, then a psychiatrist at the Boston Psychopathic Hospital, noticed that levels of grief resembled in their symptoms levels of mental illness. He began to recruit survivors of the disaster for a long-term study. The stages of grief (similar in some ways to the stages of grief in a dying person as identified by Kubler-Ross) were, as we know, first denial (oh no!), next blame, next self-blame, and finally authentic grief, deep sobbing which wracks the whole body. Lindemann tried to develop a whole theory of psychopathology based on the defense against loss, believing that people could lock into denial or a blaming or self-blaming stage and not get beyond it, resulting in schizophrenia, paranoia, or psychotic depression. This may be why the Lindemann study isn't famous. As a global theory of psychopathology it works a little, but not much. As a study of the grieving process it was very accurate and enormously helpful. The stages don't necessarily follow each other in an orderly fashion. When you work with a grieving person you discover that they jump back and forth between one stage and another, or in the case of a long terminal illness, you may find that most of the grief work was done by the survivors before the person died.

Grief work is regarded by everyone as the parish minister's job, but psychiatrists are still worried that we will do it badly. This for good reason. It would be interesting to study when it was that it became un-Christian to grieve. Jesus grieved. The Old Testament, particularly the psalms, is like a record of grief. The Jews have always grieved. Most cultures grieve and, like the Jews, have a culturally defined grieving ritual. The Puritans seem to have been the culprits in America. Gravestones are too ambiguous to be very helpful but they suggest that those with the strongest doctrine of election grieved the least. Their gravestones are more likely to be reminders that we all may die at any moment and better be ready. Nineteenth-century New England gravestones for children either show a sentimental belief in the resurrection (the child who was but a bud on earth is now flowering in heaven) or a stark, terrible, naked, despairing grief that makes one's flesh crawl; it is almost a curse.

Whenever it happened, certainly in the first half of this century ministers tended to arrive with cheerful consolation and reassuring prayers. They tried at once to convince the griever that he or she shouldn't be sad; the dead person is, after all, in the presence of our Lord. This is all very well in its intention, which is appropriate, but it ignores the pain of the person grieving. The dead person may be happily in heaven, but the dead person is no longer here near the friend, lover, or spouse, who, in however ambivalent a way, loved that person. Consolation doesn't touch grief. But once the person finishes grieving, it is appropriate consolation which may make a difference in the life of that person from then on. It was the timing, not the content of the consolation, which was so destructive.

Ministers trained in grief work (and very quickly the Lindemann model spread into the received wisdom of pastoral care through C.P.E.) would arrive at the door of the bereaved not distanced by cheerful prayers, but without defenses, displaying their own strong feelings of empathy. They would immediately embrace the bereaved and say something like, "Oh my God, what a terrible thing has happened to you" — especially if the loss was sudden, traumatic and unexpected, like a car accident or a suicide. Here again, transference is essential and must be established quickly. The whole point of grief work is to break through the various ego defenses people use to keep from regressing — denial, blame, self-blame — to the pre-verbal stage of infancy where loss has wounded the most basic ground of trust and safety and the need for total somatic expression can be touched and freed.

Here countertransference, the minister's own reactions that she or he brings to death, is part of the therapeutic process. What is needed is a non-anxious presence, a parental presence, yet someone who shows some empathy even to the point of sharing the grief itself. The pastor will no doubt be anxious, and in attempting to cover up the anxiety, stiff and undemonstrative as well. I have helped people grieve when I was wearing clericals and when I was dressed informally. I find my anxiety disappears more quickly in clericals because my role is immediately established and my relationship to this particular grieving person quickly recalled and, for a reason I suspect is generational, I feel more free to be physically demonstrative in clericals. There is often a great deal of chaos and turbulence when one arrives at the door of the bereaved, particularly if the death has been sudden or traumatic. It is helpful in the midst of friends and neighbors of the bereaved to be immediately identifiable, to become the non-anxious center of this turbulence as it plays itself out.

If you embrace the bereaved and express something empathic, "Oh my God! What a terrible thing!" it is likely that your normal range of feelings will return and you may weep. A strong and various flow of emotion in the pastor may often break open the grief of the bereaved and hasten her grieving process. But if, for whatever reason, a pastor remains emotionally tight, then clericals, a parental role, prayers, and encouraging any expressions of grief is enough to be helpful.

You begin by requesting the bereaved to tell you what happened. Whenever he begins to weep and the narrative breaks down, you wait, touch, hold and encourage the weeping. Weeping is not sobbing, however. As the weeping subsides, pray with the bereaved, asking God for the strength to proceed, and then get back to the narrative. It will be punctuated with cries of denial ("I can't believe it happened"), blame ("That goddamned resident never even gave her a spinal tap"), self-blame ("I knew the brakes were lousy, I should have had the brakes fixed"). One never comments on the content of these defenses. The bereaved may express rage and blame toward the deceased, towards a spouse, a doctor, anyone.

Don't try to argue rationally with these comments, which are all attempts to create a rational world out of the chaos of loss.

In the best of all cases, the sobbing will come, even screaming and writhing. Try to hold the bereaved, uttering support for the grief.

This is, as I say, the best of all cases. When the sobbing subsides the bereaved will become rational. Color will return to the face. The bereaved will often be able to sleep without sedatives and to cope with funeral arrangements and the other demanding details surrounding death. The process can take four or five hours.

Try to keep liquor and sedatives out of this process. They will slow it down or stop it completely.

Usually, this grieving process will be partial. There may be no more than slight weeping. You may have to leave with the person still threatening lawsuits or full of self-blame or still angry at the deceased. But the process has begun if the narrative has been completed. Keep working for weeping and other expressions of grief as you plan the funeral with the bereaved. If there are children, let them be present and encourage them to talk. If no one else does, pick them up and hug them occasionally. Above all, drop in to see the family from time to time in the weeks to come.

During these visits consolation begins to be appropriate and it is then that questions of meaning and theology should be addressed. In the meantime say clearly to the bereaved, "Don't try to make sense out of this. It is senseless now. Later we can try to make sense out of it."

Well, so much for counseling theory applied to the specifics of individual loss of someone close through death. It is probably the most important intervention a parish minister is expected to make. Of all human crises, it is most exclusively the minister's professional turf. Yet a fair number of ministers are simply unable to cope with it because they themselves have not come to terms with loss and grief. If a parishioner calls to announce the death of a family member, there are ministers who will immediately try to arrange the funeral over the phone. I have known ministers who had great trouble doing funerals at all, and pleaded with other ministers in the vicinity to take them. If there is one thing a seminarian preparing for ordination must do, it is to come to terms with death, loss, and grief. Indeed, there is growing evidence that any human being who has not come to terms with death, loss, and grief will live a less than meaningful and coherent life.

In the past, the culture was pervaded with lessons about living with death, loss and grief without denying them. Although in the last two decades we have tried to cope on a psychological level with the denial of death, our empirical obsessions have kept us, as a culture, embarrassed at the prospect of retrieving old notions of immortality, or eternal life or death and resurrection. It is hard for the empirically trained intellect, in fact it is almost impossible, to remythologize. What has been reduced to "nothing but" superstition, or wishful thinking, or mere anecdote cannot suddenly be restored to its mythic function and power, simply by putting the intellect in reverse. Reality addressed empirically or mythically is the same reality, at least for monotheists. We're committed to this by faith. Yet these quite different modes of perceptual address have different consequences. In the end we perceive reality empirically in order to manage it; we perceive reality mythically to discover our place in it. With our "grief work" and thanatology and the like, we are attempting to manage death. We have neglected to understand our place as mortal yet conscious beings in a context seen empirically as random and careless and entropic, yet mythically as God's, as significant, as an expression of infinite love.

Christianity as a liberating agent liberates first from the power of death. All human freedom, as Martin Luther King understood so well, depends first on freedom from the conviction that death has the last word on the human condition and that survival exhausts the meaning of salvation.

But loss is not simply a matter of loss through death. In times of rapid social change, loss becomes a powerful metaphor for a recurrent human experience. I mentioned earlier the loss due to transiency.

A suburban parish minister is handed a pew slip from a new parishioner at the church door after a service. It is good policy to call on Monday. Often you will discover, when you ring the bell and the door opens, a woman still in a dressing gown at two in the afternoon, who lets you in and tries to smile, tries to be welcoming, but is clearly very depressed, very flat, and registers very little affect. You notice that the T.V. is on. Hyperactive small kids are tearing around. The rug isn't down. The curtains aren't up. Things are a mess.

What you are faced with is grief and loss. This woman has lost her friends, her neighborhood, possibly her job with all its relationships, her sitters, her doctor, her obstetrician, in fact, a whole life. Your job as a minister is right there, at that very moment, to get her talking about what she has lost. You may very well find the conversation moving through the classical stages of grief. Denial ("Isn't this a lovely town!"), blame ("Sometimes I think the company plans this, just waits until you're really established, you've found a decent child care center, you have your real estate license and then says now's the time to transfer him"), to self-blame ("I don't know why I let it get to me like this. I bargained for it when I married him") and finally to tears and weeping. Then the color returns, the voice becomes animated, and finally the conversation turns to the details of starting a new life.

I once gave a talk on transiency to the staff of an ecumenical counseling clinic in a suburb and after that the clinic added transiency issues to its intake procedure. The director told me a year later that the result had been a significant reduction in the clinic's case load.

For men, of course, the loss of a job, being laid off or fired, creates the same kind of psychic turbulence and pain. Often the first thing a fired or laid off man does is to quit coming to church. If you call on him, he may tell you that he feels like a loser. He's ashamed to be at church with all those winners.

Black churches are very different. Many of them have a place in the service where they invite visitors or new parishioners to stand up and introduce themselves. There is a ritual of bringing greetings that comes right out of the New Testament. "Brothers and sisters, I bring you greetings from your brothers and sisters at Hope Baptist in Birmingham, Alabama. We've just moved here and we're staying with my sister Mrs. Walter Gray until we can find a house and a job. I was doing roofing in Birmingham and I'd appreciate it if you'd tell me if you hear about any work in that line, or if you know about a home that's available." After the service parishioners make a beeline for the new arrivals and invite the family to lunch. This is real "shared ministry" built in to Black Christian culture. Most white churches just don't have this level of trust. The fact that it is a part of the liturgy removes some of the embarassment.

The fact that this mode of dealing with the loss that results from transiency and uprootedness is built into Black Christian culture liturgically, is what I mean when I say that the central task of pastoral care is the construction of a world made meaningful and purposeful as it expresses itself in Christian symbol and metaphor. The family metaphor inherent in the address of brother and sister, the New Testament custom of bringing greetings from a congregation in one place to another, the invitation to a meal with its eucharistic implications—all of these things address and heal the injuries to one's deep sense of the loss of the kind of familiarity and safety one equates with being at home. But I would also insist that what happens in this case goes beyond some sort of psychological euphoria, some momentary good feeling of being safe, and moves over into the cognitive, the rational and the ethical. It is a basis for human freedom.

White Christians invited by Black churches in the South to join in the civil rights movement there arrived from the safety and ease of their normal lives into an atmosphere of pure menace. They were worried about their capacity for non-violence and, of course, frightened by the possibility for violence towards them that lurked everywhere in their new environment. They had said goodbye to friends and family with the fear—a highly exaggerated fear, but real nonetheless—that they might not see them again. The rite of inclusion in Black worship services, the ritualized bringing of greetings from their congregation in the North, the warm welcome and meal that followed, all of these things together were taken out into the street. What they were asked to do and called to do made sense, powerful ethical sense. It freed them from their deep fear and ambivalence to exercise real moral agency, to work at the construction of a moral world in the dangerous political environment of the times. But even more important, they were prepared to do this within the context of nonviolence, a context which assumes the value and redeemable humanity of those who provoke or attack you.

People whose real or anticipated loss has never been addressed, whose life has no continuity, no narrative line, but is simply a string of discontinuous events, are primarily concerned with strategies for avoiding more loss, with hanging on to what they have or getting more of it. And what they have in place of continuity and purpose is too often money or prestige, or power, or despair. More money is spent in the United States on private security arrangements than on public law enforcement.

But how can parish ministry or pastoral care address this pervasive sense of loss? How can it use its understanding of the psychodynamics of loss in its construction of a theological world? I have given one example, but it is hard to translate a practice of one culture in some literal way into another culture. The resistance will be considerable.

Perhaps a key is for the parish minister simply to be more aware of the pervasive dynamics of loss and change. The most obvious example of this in the Episcopal Church was the change that took place in the late seventies from the 1928 Book of Common Prayer to the current Prayer Book authorized in 1972. Particularly for lifelong Episcopalians, the 1928 Prayer Book was clearly more than a book. They were baptized with it and so were their children; their parents were buried with it; they themselves were probably married with it. Crucial moments of their lives are associated with it. As a symbol in the Episcopal Church the power of the Book of Common Prayer may be even greater than that of the Bible, since so much of it is from the Bible or interpretive of the Bible. So for some Episcopalians the change was like having a leg amputated and replaced by a viable artificial limb. One is grateful for the new, but it doesn't exactly replace the old; one forgets that the old was amputated for good reason. It had lost its function. One remembers it as perfectly one's own, and one feels the loss painfully as one limps along on the new, trying to get used to it.

The 1928 Prayer Book, with much of its language still the product of the original genius of Cranmer, was written for a people who to all intents and purposes believed that the world was the center of the universe and God's concern. God, not entropy, ruled the creation. Human beings were a separate creation, made to rule over all else as creatures in the image of God; in this respect, however fallen, they were rational and free to choose whether to obey God's will or not. The '28 Prayer Book was written for a people whose primary temptation and sin was pride.

Aesthetically, poetically, as literature it was magnificent. Its language was written for the ear. For priests celebrating the Eucharist, the service was sheer music to read aloud. But it did not address people whose primary sin and temptation were the failure of self-esteem and the sense of meaninglessness that went with it. The book's whole theological thrust was penitential and Anselmian, based on one of Paul's several metaphors for the atonement and a feudal legal system. So much of the book was an assault on human self-esteem. For those few who listened to the words and understood them, it was not helpful to have what little self-esteem they had left assaulted. It had to be changed.

For those who loved the 1928 Prayer Book's music and symbolic action, while ignoring its theology or quietly altering the words in their heads, the loss was painful. Its associations with crucial moments in their lives made its loss more painful yet. But the language of the new Prayer Book was workmanlike, if it did grate on the ear, and its theology was acceptable—or more acceptable. However, the change from the old book was experienced as pure loss by many and a crisis developed as parish ministers tried to effect it.

The most effective way, we were told, was preparation and education. Trial use books came out one after another and were used on special occasions, or for the time being, as adult education courses and sermons were used to explain the superiority of the new services and the theological reasons for the change. Those ministers who did this fared far better than those who didn't, but the results were still spotty for a long time with much anger and rebellion and people cutting pledges or moving to parishes which held out for the 1928.

Those parishes which met the least resistance to the change were those whose ministers used the preparation and education procedure as a time also to grieve the loss of the old book. They shared their own attachment to the book, told their parishioners how it had got them through rough times or helped them celebrate their experiences of grace, praised the eloquence and beauty of its prose, and the profundity of its great prayers — all of which were going to be kept in the new book.

My favorite incident in the great prayer book war was when a minister I knew who had done all of the above finally met the day of truth. The final edition of the new prayer book in hard cover had arrived. He placed one next to each copy of the 1928 version in the pews on Saturday night. At the Sunday Eucharist, which he celebrated from the new book, he preached one last sermon on the glories of the old, which ended with an invitation to all parishioners to take home a copy of the 1928 to put by their bed for their private devotions. The grieving was over. The continuity of each person's spiritual life was maintained or at least not ignored, the loss was grieved, and the new Prayer Book accepted without argument.

I don't bring this up as a success story, but as an example of how counseling theory can be applied to the issue of parish change, where change is understood as loss. Here a therapeutic insight is used not for the sake of avoiding conflict, but for helping to construct a world of sense and purpose, which is the proper focus of pastoral care.

Alas, the new Prayer Book along with the educational process that emphasized the importance of its language and theology had results that few expected. It turned out that a large number of Episcopalians continued to find the Book of Common Prayer an assault upon their self-esteem, if for totally different reasons.

I am referring to the many women who found in the language of the new book a curious linguistic ignoring of their existence, along with the theological assumption that God is male. When the services were in Latin or Jacobean prose, really written for another age, no one paid much attention to the language on the level of intellectual content. But now the language was written for us to understand and we could no longer ignore it.

However, the feminists are right, I think, in saying that male pronouns and male metaphors for God are not just discrete cases of language that fail to include and can simply be changed to make the services more "inclusive."

These metaphors reflect a total religious male patriarchal paradigm that pervades every aspect of the church. Now I'm not going to get into this incredibly complex matter here. Yet this paradigm belongs to a subsistence society with minimal technology, the society lived in by all but a tiny segment of rich people up until the nineteenth century. It was the agreed-upon way that men and women made sense out of their life together. It was a question of "compared to what?"

Today this paradigm is too anomalous, too full of conflict and injustice, to make sense out of a great deal of our life together as men and women. Yet, as is painfully obvious, there is no new paradigm to take its place. It is still a question of "compared to what?"

The reason I mention this painful issue here is because what we are dealing with is loss, and for those who want to deal with this most profound of paradigm changes, some understanding of the place of the grieving process in change is essential. When people are asked to give up their way of making sense out of life, for them it is the same as being asked to go crazy. For the patriarchal religious paradigm, this is every bit as true for women as it is for men. As in the case of loss by death, the more ambivalence one has felt toward the person who died, the more complex and painful and difficult may be the grieving process. The person whose love for the deceased was strongest and least ambivalent will often let go sooner, and so will more quickly recover a new and significant relationship to the lost person.

For this is the theological function of the church in loss. No loss is grieved until one has established a new relationship to the lost object, whether the object be a homeland, a spouse, a child or a paradigm.

In his novel *More Die of Heartbreak*, Saul Bellow takes the title from the response of one character, a scientist of international reputation, to a reporter who asks him to comment on the dangers of radiation to the human race. "More die of heartbreak," he replies. Bellow is the great chronicler of cultural and generational discontinuity in Western society. His heroes emerge from a rich, coherent, sustaining culture into eminence in the great world only to find themselves alienated and grieving. They struggle to recapture some relationship to the sustaining culture from which they came and which is now lost to them forever. His characters often have a vision of the holy, the sacred, but it serves only to alienate them from the dangerous, hypercompetitive, chaotic world in which they find themselves.

Although Bellow focuses on the American Jewish experience which he knows intimately, his work is a metaphor for the American middle-class experience in general. We move a lot. We often "succeed." We surpass the achievements of our parents. We "outgrow" our communities of birth and childhood. We become mobile — upwardly and laterally. We break one attachment after another. But we don't grieve. Instead we grow nostalgic, sentimental, reactionary. We mumble about a return to "basics." Or we adapt to life as pure process, and find what satisfaction we can find in pure technique, in what is often called today the "pursuit of excellence."

The nostalgia, the "back to basics," is often a good inclination gone wrong. It reflects the normal human desire to address and be addressed by the holy. The unrelenting fragmentation and discontinuity of American middle-class life again and again leaves us alienated and separate, marginal, bereft of any sense of belonging apart from our work, where our belonging is based on our utility.

The church is most the church of Jesus Christ when it intentionally places itself on this same margin, not existing as a cheerful and successful part of the killing aimlessness and greed of what has become the American social norm. From the margin the church can submit the disintegrated culture around us to the penetrating vision of Scripture. It can find things in our past, things we have lost or discarded and now grieve, which can be retrieved and integrated into a new whole which it can bless. Many things in the past which we discarded because they seemed to serve us badly, we miss because the needs they met so badly are now not met at all. Obligations we happily abandoned in the belief that they were met by government or education or science, we now discover are met by none of these. We realize that many will suffer until we are willing to face and reassess and reflect upon these obligations in the light of Scripture, so that we can reappropriate them as we attempt to build a moral community.

For individuals, as for the culture of which they are a part, the loss of one's narrative, the cumulative discontinuities in one's story, need to be grieved. What has been lost through death or transiency or even rational decision must be addressed again. A new relationship must be established with them that has narrative coherence, as Scripture has coherence based not simply on aesthetic imagination, but on God's grace, God's providence.

If feminists would look at the reactions of both men and women to their assault on the patriarchal paradigm of the Prayer Book, they would notice first denial. "Oh no.

There's nothing wrong with the language. It all refers to both man and woman." Then blame. "Those people are just trying to call attention to themselves and make a mess of everything." Third, self-blame, which takes the form of withdrawal, separation and depression. The feminists themselves tend to follow the same pattern, locking into blame after they break through denial. Neither side has reached any profound felt sense of what has been lost, and neither side is attempting to work at a new relationship to the lost object. Actually, neither side can. It would require a joint effort.

A final example of where loss understood in terms of counseling theory can be helpful is in the matter of a change of rector or parish minister. As seniors approach the end of their stay at seminary they are taught how to "terminate," how to say goodbye, how to work through not only their anxiety about leaving, but their feelings of loss at departing from the web of relationships developed in three years.

This may even be a bit overdone for some people, since the move in this case, if one actually finds a job, is a move from insecurity to more security, from spending money to earning money, from a largely passive mode of existence to lively, spirited, purposeful activity. Many recent graduates of seminary do not feel an overwhelming need to grieve their loss. They feel more like celebrating their new freedom.

But one day, if they are ordained parish ministers, they will have to leave their first job for another. Now a good deal is said about the importance at this time of helping the parish to say goodbye, to get used in advance to the minister's departure. There are many ceremonial parties, gifts, farewell speeches, all preparing the congregation for the loss of its minister, while it is more or less assumed that all this is helping the minister, too. But often ministers are not facing their own loss at all. Instead, as professionals and as pastors *in loco parentis*, at the end of their stay in a parish most ministers are helping that parish to grieve.

One thing I am sure of. The loss of a parish for some ministers, even if they move from a parish they have not enjoyed at all to one that fulfills their most heavenly fantasies, can be deeply traumatic and even professionally damaging. A cliche of the parish ministry is this: "The first year you can do no wrong. The second year you can do no right. The third year they don't care what you do." This deeply cynical comment describes a ministry that has gone wrong from the beginning, of course. Yet it is a mistake to ignore this kind of cynicism. It may be describing something real that needs attention. Where it holds, one can conjecture that the congregation has made a strong transference to a new and grieving minister during his or her first year in the parish.

They insist that the minister be an omnipotent parent while the minister feels like a lost child. I have seen ministers during their first year preach sermons that literally punished their new congregation for not being thir old congregation. I have seen others so withdrawn and unattached that they seemed like ghosts. They simply did not respond with any vitality to anything. I have seen other ministers launch an all-out attack on a new parish to make all the same changes they made in their last parish.

The result of many of these grief reactions on the minister's part is a sense of anger and betrayal among the congregation, whose grand transferential expectations have been met either with an inappropriate response or no response at all.

The second year the minister may have emerged from grief and be able to function professionally, but faced with a negative transference so forceful that by the third year both parties have settled for the *status quo ante*. If the time is used for building trust, the process can begin again with neither side grieving or overwhelmed by transferential expectations. This is not fatal to a good and lively ministry — that is, if the minister doesn't start looking for a new job the fourth year and leave the fifth.

As for that first year, it is obviously not always as bad as I have described it, but sometimes it is fully that bad. Yet I see no way to build into the pastoral construction of a world some antidote to deal with it. Where the help should come from is from other priests or ministers in the vicinity, but so long as our model for the ordained parish minister is so entrepreneurial and competitive, this may not happen.

To my way of thinking, there is no other area of pastoral care in which counseling theory is so helpful as that of loss and change. At the heart of the whole matter is the Christian theological response to death. Without this theological ground, prepared in sermons and adult education as well as in the minister's behavior in the presence of death, all the psychological grief work in the world cannot deal with the issues of meaning and purpose, upon which depends a new relationship to the lost object. Our vocation as ordained ministers is primarily to this end.

Preaching

Once when I was on my vacation, I remember hearing a particularly unfortunate sermon in which the preacher kept referring to what he called "passive-dependent Christians." He went into some detail in order to describe Christians who, he said, believed that not only God but also the church would take care of them as if they were small children. Such people, the preacher claimed, gave little or nothing to the church, yet still expected it to provide Christian education for their children, marry and bury them, provide Sunday worship, and visit them when they were sick. These "passive-dependent Christians" pledged nothing at all, never volunteered to teach church school or carry their share of the every-member canvas. He kept repeating the words "passive-dependent" in a voice touched with vague disdain.

There is a great deal of precedent for this kind of sermon and it goes all the way back to St. Paul. It is also part of the minister's pastoral responsibilities. However most ministers find this kind of sermon a chore; some simply avoid it and the risk of sounding like a common scold that goes along with preaching such sermons. Yet if the pastor sees evidence of a fair amount of shared behavior in parish life that is destructive of actual mutuality, it should probably be addressed.

St. Paul could be quite scathing about behavior in the community that did not contribute to the common life, yet the assumption behind everything he said was that such behavior could—indeed would—be changed. Paul might even accuse his congregation of regression, of childish behavior, of needing milk rather than the meat of the mature. But he expected mature behavior, for in his practice of ministry Paul had a very robust doctrine of human freedom.

It occurs to me that this may be why I have never liked Paul very much. As one immersed in the language and habits of the therapeutic culture, I see Paul as an arrogant and oftentimes moralistic man who is always telling me how I am supposed to act and what I am supposed to believe. Yet he, unlike the preacher I heard on my vacation, never tells me who I am and then goes on to say that who I am is unacceptable. The use of the phrase "passive-dependent" suggests that I am a certain personality type, determined from my infancy, which will control certain aspects of my behavior until I die or go into counseling. Indeed, any sermon that focuses on my personality rather than my behavior is no more than scolding; it may make me feel vaguely miserable, but it will not help me change my behavior. Paul's metaphor of milk and meat, on the other hand, suggests to me that the behavior can be outgrown. The biblical image implies a freedom to change, the possibility of true metanoia as a slow, intentional, developmental process.

It might be argued today that it is not the job of the parish minister to change people's behavior. Who is this person to lecture a group of adults about how they should behave? Isn't it precisely this patriarchal or matriarchal role that leads to the infantilization of the laity? The answer to this question is simple enough. The priest has been chosen by the congregation to articulate and iterate a traditional consensus about what constitutes moral interaction among Christians. One of the few aspects of moral behavior in the parish about which there is still some consensus is the matter of stewardship of both time and money. Although the rationale for this consensus is more often based on survival than salvation, stewardship is a truly moral issue. It is a metaphor and a sacramental expression of mutual concern within the body of Christ.

I suppose that there is a question prior to and underlying the issue of how counseling theory should or should not be used in preaching, and that has to do with the relationship of preaching to pastoral care and parish ministry.

First, when I speak of preaching here, I am speaking of the cumulative effect of preaching Sunday after Sunday, year after year, to a congregation that is relatively stable — stable, that is, relative to the demographic or economic situation of the community within which it exists. It is this cumulative effect that is so important, yet preaching is often thought of as the preparation of discrete sermons, each an occasion in itself.

Even when this is the preaching philosophy of the preacher, a cumulative effect will be present. The preacher's theology will, over the years, become manifest to the congregation and may even be adopted by a number of parishioners as a way to make sense out of their existence. Or it may turn out that the preacher has no theology at all, just an overlay of theological cliches to give the odor of sanctity to a simple empirical view of life. This, too, will affect the nature of pastoral care understood as the construction of a world.

Yet the world constructed is more likely to reflect the empiricism than the pious overlay. There are churches in the United States that are almost entirely pragmatic and instrumental, rationalized down to the last committee. Their public relations efforts are generated by a professional firm. They have an Olympic-sized pool, an indoor running track, a health food bar, a fully computerized office, and all the rest. Such churches tend to be fundamentalist in their preaching, although interestingly enough their counseling centers, if they have them, will dispense therapeutic insights and solutions even though anything smelling of the therapeutic will be castigated from the pulpit as Satanic or part of a Communist plot.

The example of such churches may seem irrelevant to an Episcopalian, but they demonstate a similar conflict; in the Episcopal Church, the sermons preached on Sunday morning are just as likely to be at odds with the parish world that has actually been constructed. From the pulpit come exhortations to love, to be just, to be compassionate, to be inclusive, while the fund raising methods, the election of a vestry, or the calling of a minister can be as harshly competitive as anything found in the corporate world.

The primary purpose of preaching is to let the Gospel be known, apprehended, and taken as the good news of our salvation through Jesus Christ, the news that love has overcome death and we are ultimately safe.

But if we begin to accept this good news as true, then it has consequences for how we live our lives together. Our liberation from bondage to sin and death not only makes us feel good, it also affects our corporate life. This, then, is the function of preaching in pastoral care: edification, building up, the construction of a world.

I think that the modern church has made a great mistake in interpreting this work of edification too empirically, seeing it in terms of building actual communities within the parish. Through insights borrowed from group dynamics and human potential techniques, we attempted to build joyful, generous, open, warm, and healthy communities in our parishes. Where we succeeded, we built very exclusive communities for white middle-class college graduates. To have a sense of belonging in such communities was to commit oneself to the values and rules delivered to the parish through the preaching of the minister—who was fresh from this lab or that institute. Those who accepted this model benefited from it in many ways. They did become more sensitive to others, particularly in a group interaction. Many discovered their feelings, able to name them and to be conscious of them for the first time, and so could live with them without being tyrannized by them. Some people learned a kind of self-acceptance that made them less defensive and devious in dealing with their neighbors, and they learned to celebrate this community joyfully.

Where they were successful, such parishes served the personal well-being of parishioners as well as the health of their families. They may even have contributed to the good of the greater society by sending people into it who knew who they were, who were sensitive to others and "felt good" about themselves. However these people did not have any particular ethical orientation, or, indeed, any particular values beyond the therapeutic goals of adaptivity, maturity, and the reduction of conflict— free smooth functioning with, perhaps, a little kindness thrown in. They were nice, pleasant, happy people, who seemed to prosper in their love and work, which was no small thing; as Freud said, it is the basic sign of health.

Preaching within this parish model tended to be couched in the language of personal development and growth, all with a pious overlay. It is surprisingly easy to go through the New Testament and find all kinds of scriptural texts that seem to confirm counseling theory about human interaction. I remember two especially popular passages. "Be angry and sin not," from Ephesians 4:26 meant "Express your negative feelings in order to get rid of them," while "If . . . you suddenly remember your brother has a grievance against you . . . first go and make peace with your brother" from Matthew 5:24 was a directive about conflict. Don't avoid it. Confront it and work it through.

To lift isolated exhortations from the New Testament and use them outside of any context whatever as a bolster for therapeutic insights is a fundamentalism in search of proof texts. Such preaching, however, confirmed and maintained and rationalized and interpreted the world that was being constructed by adult education curricula, church school teacher training, counseling and even the committees and task groups of the parish.

During the early sixties, which was the heyday of this model, very little serious attention was given in preaching (or any other way) to the community beyond the parish, or to social justice on the national scene. There were vivid exceptions to this, of course, but insularity was by and large the norm.

When the civil rights movement really began to make itself felt, it made its first impact through preaching and the results were unexpected. As Don Browning likes to point out, ordained ministers tended to assume that counseling theory was somehow contained and held in check by the moral and ethical values of the parish. They took for granted that the objective and "value-free" interchanges essential to counseling took place within a traditional moral context that would hold, rather than

Brenda Memorial Library
The Salvadon Army
79
School for Officers' Training
Suffern, N.Y.

offering a whole new morality. These ministers were simply unaware of the extent to which therapeutic culture had taken over the moral and ethical values of the parish.

Seen from a New Testament perspective, racism is a simple ethical problem. It goes against the very heart of the Gospel's revelation of the nature of God. It is so wrong as to be blasphemous. To many ministers this seemed so obvious that saying so hardly seemed controversial.

Yet the reaction of many Episcopalians in the pews to this new turn toward social ethics was confused, and led to conflict within the parish. "Of course racism is wrong, but I don't know any colored people. They are not a part of my life. What does this have to do with me?" Leaving aside the solid block of hardcore racists in the church, who were as opposed to counseling theory as they were to racial equality, the more usual reaction in white suburban churches to preaching for racial justice was likely to be, "Don't bother me with things over which I have no control. I am concerned with being a healthy person, making a difference where I am. Your bringing politics and ideology into the pulpit makes me feel bad about things I can't really change."

The "I didn't do it, I can't change it, don't blame me" attitude was itself tied to certain assumptions of counseling theory. A person who showed an intense concern for matters beyond the range of that person's family, work and social environment was, as they say, "having problems" —with relationships in the family, at work, or in their social life. People influenced by the human potential movement would say of social activism, "It's pure projection. Just taking over our inner conflicts and projecting them on society and trying to resolve them there." This kind of thinking led to easy trivialization of social issues and some parish ministers lost their credibility in the pulpit through the adoption of attitudes which they themselves had encouraged and fostered.

Now in some cases preaching laid the minister open to this kind of criticism. Preachers would blame and rant at their congregations when they found that they were without interest in social justice. Sermons became predictable and boring and, in one sense, neurotic; they were accomplishing the opposite of what they were intended to do, hardening people to the issue of racial justice and creating a well of hostility towards the preacher.

On a superficial level, the criticisms were partially true. It is inherent in the very nature of imagination and empathy to be distorted to some degree by individual experience. But imagination and empathy are the heart of ethical commitment, and where they are naively and uncritically accepted as sufficient reason for ethical action ("I feel it should be obvious to anyone that what I am doing is right"), then they are hugely untrustworthy as a source of motivation.

Ironically enough, other ministers who were well trained in counseling theory and group process provided a new kind of social activist leadership. They exercised leadership that was committed and assertive, yet sensitive to group process and to the pain and conflict of individuals, including the adversary. These ministers knew about projection; they were aware of the dangers of escaping from one's own real problems by hurling oneself into the movement. They were constantly checking themselves and one another out on their motivations to keep them from fouling up the real purpose of the movement.

One of the great preachers of our time was Martin
Luther King. Sometimes we forget that he got his training
at Boston University School of Theology, for years the
most counseling oriented seminary in the United States.
The first time I heard King preach was in 1961 to a
congregation of students at Williams College. The sermon
King preached relied heavily on his psychological
sophistication, dealing primarily with the question of
balance in the inner life and the importance of self-esteem.
Race was hardly mentioned, although at that time he was
in the middle of leading the Montgomery bus boycott.

But self-esteem was mentioned, and what made King
such a great leader was this single concept taken from
counseling theory and assimilated into a biblical theology.
And I think it was rightly and appropriately assimilated,
because Jesus, in his encounters with the poor and the
sick, was intensely aware of their self-regard. Jesus did not
tell them how good they were, he simply loved them and
they began to want to become good. Think of the disbelief
expressed by the Samaritan woman at the well in John 4.
She was astonished that Jesus even spoke to her, and how
animated, witty, and theologically acute she became as
she realized that Jesus, the Messiah, was speaking to her
in full knowledge of who she was and how she had lived
her life.

I think it is important to notice that Ronald Reagan,
another very successful leader, has always been aware of
the importance of self-esteem, but in an ethical and
religious vacuum. Instead of confirming the divine image
in people, with its potential for responding to the
demands of justice and love, American leadership
confirms the greedy, violent, selfish, competitive behavior
of people, tells them it is okay, the American way. Both

King and Reagan have been extraordinarily effective in addressing people to quite different ends. Their effectiveness lies in understanding that there has been and continues to be a chronic national questioning of self-esteem. Indeed the issue of self-esteem seems to be an important one in all developed countries; it is inevitably tied to science and technology and the empirical world-view that goes with them. Where all important issues are set as problems to be solved, and the bottom line can or should always be quantified, it is hard to see the importance of one human being—if only because nothing really important is solved in life and, we are constantly being told, there are far too many human beings on this planet. In essence, we are simply complicated animals pitted against each other and the rest of creation for survival, and our rational nature is a sham. Where this reductionist, scientific self-definition is endemic in a culture, it is not hard to see why self-regard might become an issue, and why we might listen to anyone who even suggested that we were of some value. This need of ours lies at the center of cult dynamics as well.

All of this has significance for preaching. I once heard one of the more famous preachers in the Episcopal Church say in a lecture on preaching, "When I preach, I always go for a conviction." This is the classical mode of preaching for conversion. One convicts one's listeners in the congregation, defines them as hopeless sinners, alienated from God and neighbor, and then presents them with a God who would care for them if only they would let him. I say "him" advisedly, because for these preachers God is a strict father who has been disobeyed or ignored.

People still like this kind of preaching, but for curious reasons. They like it first of all because it defines the way they feel about themselves and so confirms their sanity. They learn that they are not the only people who feel this way. Then, since their belief in the God who has saved or will save them from this state is minimal, belief for them is empirical, totally dependent on "the facts." They hear a curious message that it is all right, indeed, simply part of the human condition to be the sinners that they are. There is no need to change. They see not only their sinful condition confirmed, but their sinful behavior as well. They see no need or even possibility for repentance. People enjoy this kind of preaching because, as they interpret it, it makes no real demands on them. It also helps to make preachers feel like prophets, strengthening their own self-image as people of integrity.

This issue of self-regard is absolutely critical to parish ministry today, yet it is also one of the most theologically difficult issues the church faces. Counseling theory sees self-esteem as lying at the heart of all healthy and adaptive behavior towards self and others. Yet to the extent that this theory is derived from Freud, it assumes that self-esteem, feeling comfortable with oneself, having a healthy ego, whatever you want to call it, is based on basic trust, the result of a first year of adequate parenting. Another assumption goes along with this—that when we're talking about successful therapy we're talking about clients whose basic trust is intact, clients whose pathology does not occur at such a deep level. A psychoanalyst like Hans Kohut maintains that in treating disorders stemming from damage at this level of trust, you must work out strategies that avoid getting into this deepest and best defended level of the unconscious. Otherwise, the therapy can be more dangerous to the patient than the defenses themselves. I have even heard a Jesuit spiritual director say that a person damaged at the trust level can never learn really to pray. I think this is silly, but I would agree that it is dangerous for people to practice a mode of prayer which demands the obliteration of the ego, if their ego isn't in very good shape. Whether this kind of prayer, common to Tibetan Buddhism, is an appropriate form of Christian prayer is something which should be examined more closely than I think it has been.

At various times in its history Christianity has looked at the self in different ways. The gospels' primary statement about self is in the second dominical commandment, "Thou shalt love thy neighbor as thy self," yet elsewhere in the New Testament we are urged to die to ourselves, to deny ourselves, to humble ourselves. The Pharisee who prayed in the synagogue before the tax collector, prayed "with himself." The New Testament also uses "self" as we would use "ego." The prodigal son comes to himself. Peter in Acts comes to himself. Jesus' family say that he is "beside himself." Here the word self is defined as the sane and good core of the person, the real, conscious, unique center. Yet according to Bruno Bettelheim, the German word translated into the English word "ego" really means "soul" — not some sharp-eyed, objective, scientific core of personality, but the unique whole of a person in balance.

All of this gets translated into another internal argument of Christianity, the argument between agape and eros, between faith and works. Where the self is seen as bad, "selfish," greedy, concupiscent, and above all proud, personal piety is based on agape and faith. One surrenders to the love of God by faith. Works, even pious works of prayer and charity, do not help. If you believe Anselm or even Karl Barth, there is nothing about the self worth redeeming. The fact of its having been made in the image of God is irrelevant compared to the enormity of Adam's sin. Our salvation is entirely in God's hands. In the extreme Calvinist position even our response to God's love is in God's hands.

Where the emphasis is put on the self's similarity to the image and likeness of God, where the self has intrinsic value simply as a creature of God and sin is understood not as a genetic inheritance from Adam, but as a form of captivity to Satan and the kingdom of death, piety can follow at least two ways. According to Anders Nygren in his book *Agape and Eros*, these ways are erotic and nomic. Both are self-centered, human centered. Eros piety evaluates everything on the basis of its helpfulness in leading us to God. We are loving in order to become closer to God, we pray and follow an ascetic path to come closer to God. Everything we touch is used in our spiritual quest to become perfect, or perhaps perfectly ourselves in becoming more like God. Nothing is valued for its own sake, or even for Christ's sake, but only for its usefulness to us in our spiritual quest. The nomic variation on this theme is to make Christianity the new law, which is basically the old law but more rigorous. Anybody can love one's neighbors. Love your enemy. Anyone can fast in public, let's see you do it in private. Anyone can keep from committing adultery, but can you keep from thinking about sex at all?

Nygren calls this nomic strain the Jewish influence, and the erotic strain, Greek. He believes that true Christianity is a religion of agape.

True agape Christianity is based on dying to the worthless self, submitting wholly to God's grace and letting it fill our whole being. Out of gratitude we let it enable us to love others as God loves us, with a love that has no motive but our gratitude to God. We do not love others because it gets us into heaven or because loving the good, the true, and the beautiful in others provides basic training in loving God. We simply love them, however ugly or stupid they are; we care what happens to them. We want justice for them; we want to keep them from evil and suffering; we want to serve them. We do this cheerfully, out of the knowledge that God loves us not because of ourselves, but in spite of ourselves.

Agape was shoved down our throats in seminary. The important thing, the dean told me, was the purification of the motive, by which he meant getting every bit of eros out of our agape until it was clean as a whistle. Yet this involved a contradiction: the very attempt to rid our agape of eros was obviously either an erotic or nomic process, an attempt to save ourselves by works. The place of prayer in agape was logically unclear if it went beyond asking God to do what it was God's nature to do anyway. Certainly we didn't seek God's companionship; God had already sought out ours.

A Buddhist friend and contemporary of mine, a former Christian who had often been preached to by my generation about the glory of agape, once said to me, "The trouble with Christianity is that it doesn't teach you how to be good." Agape Christianity as it was preached in the fifties really had no place for human goodness. It was dead set against preaching any sort of moral conduct since this preaching assumed that people could be good by an act of the will. We were made good only by the grace of God and the extent to which we submitted to it.

To meet this theology, a book came straight out of counseling theory and C.P.E. called *Man's Need and God's Actions*, written by an Episcopal priest named Reuel

Howe. This book did not deny the agape doctrine of God's love for human beings, but it saw all human love as evidence of God's love, and human community as the most reliable channel of and witness to this love. God's love comes as an answer to human need through human beings. The human need for God's love is all-acceptable, indeed a given part of being human, and God's love came to meet this need through other human beings. It is not hard to see that Howe's doctrine of love was a mixture of agape and eros with a new mixture of humanism. God's love depends on human love for its expression and comes as an answer to human need, not in spite of human sin. *Man's Need and God's Action* was a good book, a mixture of Tillich and Buber and Howe, which anyone could read and most Episcopalians did. It gave consistency to preaching in Episcopal churches for a decade.

This theology also lent itself too easily to a theology of counseling theory. Before long the theological dimensions of the book were either trivialized or forgotten in many parishes, and the accent put heavily on community as an expression of human love in the name of Christ, a kind of minimalist Christianity. In some cases this in turn evolved into a kind of human potential, I'm-okay-you're-okay health spa masquerading as a parish. In others, a basically valid and serious Christianity was watered down, and preaching became a series of self-help lectures with an orthodox Christian sermon added on towards the end. As I look back on it, preachers had trouble finding a way to preach the Gospel with any power that did not depend on assaulting the self-esteem of their parishioners.

Now let me suggest a preaching theology which contains both a biblical edge and insights from counseling theory, one that helps people alter their behavior while maintaining their self-esteem. First of all, some basic theological assumptions. Human beings are made in the image of God, but their consciousness of their mortality, their knowledge of the difference between themselves as creatures and God, their creator, makes them captive to Satan, to the fear of death. Sin, then, is this captivity, this bondage. It is nothing inherently evil in ourselves. The power of sin lies in our consciousness of our mortality and of ourselves; we alone of the creation possess it. What is most God-like about us is also what causes us to sin. What frees us from our D.N.A. makes us the captives of language and culture, removing us from the rest of creation but giving us dominion over it.

Language, the word, gives us power. Our power to name gives us to a degree the power to control, but at the same time the word, the symbol is not the thing, the map is not the territory, and our view of reality is distorted at all times by our exaggerated need to exploit reality to assure our own survival, even if it is at the expense of the survival of others. This is the nature of our bondage, our sin. It is not of our essence, not at the heart of the self, where we are like God.

The atonement, what Jesus accomplished in reconciling us to himself, lay in becoming one of us, perfectly human, that is perfectly imperfect, and acting as a person free to love even at the risk of death, ignoring the claims of Satan even though he, like us, was mortal and subject to the same mortal fate of suffering and death. Through the cross Jesus overcame the power of death. The very consciousness of death which kept us in bondage, touched by the word understood as Jesus Christ, can become consciousness of resurrection and eternal life as the final end of the divine-human enterprise. Sacrificial love, love that makes holy by risking and spending itself, overcomes the kingdom of death, the rule of entropy, and frees the human race from its bondage of fear.

Working from this theology, one never in a prophetic frenzy attacks persons or groups. One speaks harshly and negatively only of specific behavior, or specific examples of bad thinking leading directly to hateful, destructive behavior. Martin Luther King seldom attacked particular people or even broad ideologies; he seldom if ever attacked racism. But King was relentless in his attack on racial discrimination, an ideology which, like apartheid, leads directly to whole patterns of behavior that derive from fear. Segregation, racial discrimination, violence, ignoring of the law — all of these forms of *behavior* were the focus of King's prophetic wrath.

With this theology one never attacks feelings, or tells people how they ought to feel. Feelings are spontaneous; they are not voluntary, unlike behavior. We are not responsible for our feelings because we have no control over them. When we damn racism, white people who either dislike or fear people of color, feel personally attacked. They cannot change their feelings on demand. They can, however, change their behavior. And there is considerable evidence that attitudinal change follows behavioral change — rather than precedes it. This is old wisdom and a part of classical Christian ethics. Ethically, we are responsible only for our behavior. Never in preaching or praying must we tell people how they are "supposed" to feel or tell them what it is bad to feel.

We do not threaten people by saying that this or that is a question of survival: "We're not talking about frills in this Every Member Canvas, we're talking survival!" "If such and such a bill doesn't get through the congress, we're dead!" The bill might have to do with funding low-cost housing and the death could be metaphorical, or it could be a bill to stop Star Wars and the survival addressed could be the literal survival of the planet. In either case, the threat to survival doesn't motivate, it either depresses and causes apathy or else it causes impulsively defensive behavior. All such allusions to survival, or winning, or success, are made under the authority of sin-and-death, the reign of Satan. People seldom behave rationally or ethically if they believe that their survival is threatened — especially if their self-esteem is at a level where they believe that they deserve to die.

When preaching from this theology, a theology that shares something with Reinhold Niebuhr, William String-fellow, and Martin Luther King, one is able to preach the choice of conversion to Jesus Christ not as salvation from being evil and sinful to becoming good, nor from anxiety and alienation to acceptance and belonging, but from captivity to freedom. It is a freedom that honors the next choice — to join in the corporate task of sanctification by participating to whatever degree in the building of a moral world.

For the average parish minister, faced with the ugly choices of a rapidly changing world, classical moral theology has proved less than useful — as has most of contemporary theology done on such a high level of abstraction and complexity.

Perhaps the first step for all serious Christians is to go beyond the belief that any choice which does not immediately serve our own survival is neurotic and self-deceptive. This, of course, is the message of the Gospel. Perfect love casts out fear. It relieves the fear of death and failure, embarrassment and error. Where our preaching can go beyond the survival aims of therapeutic theory to salvation from the bondage of sin and death, maintaining and building upon the inherent worth of the individual, then we have a basis for preaching as the very architecture of a moral world.

Parish Administration

During the fifties, when many parishes were raising funds for new church buildings, a parish minister and his vestry decided that their "plant" was too small for the rapidly growing congregation. The minister took the vestry on a retreat, where questions of fund-raising and of stewardship in general were examined prayerfully, theologically, and biblically before any decision was made. The vestry then decided to raise at least enough money to expand the church and the church school facilities, and perhaps to build a new church.

A professional fund-raiser was hired, who came highly recommended, with a record of consistent successes. Efficiently he set up the machinery, recruiting canvassers, training them in one-on-one canvassing techniques, and setting in motion a high-powered public relations campaign. The moment of truth came at an evening meeting when all the canvassers were assembled in one room. After a brief talk the fund-raiser announced, "And now, each canvasser will stand, beginning with the senior wardens, and declare his or her own pledge."

It came as a complete surprise. No one knew that this would happen. These competitive young managers and professionals squirmed as they frantically tried to assess how little they could give without appearing to be wimps.

The junior warden stood up and addressed the fund-raiser. "In my judgment this is no way for Christians to raise funds," he said. The fund-raiser looked him straight in the eye. "Do you want the money or don't you?" he asked coldly. "We want to raise some money, but not by these methods. And I don't think we'll need your services further," the junior warden said. Everyone cheered. The parish went on to canvas in a straightforward non-manipulative manner. Adequate funds for the necessary additions and alterations were raised and every pledge made was honored. Most important, the parish came through the campaign assured that their community was, in a curious way, safe. It was a place where human beings would not be coerced on the basis of their status anxiety and where their good will and commitment to the life of the parish in Christ was simply assumed. The teaching was very deep.

One of the most damaging things to happen to the self-esteem of Americans in this decade is the realization that we, as a people who practically invented "management," really don't run things very well at all. There seems to be a conflict built into our economy. Efficient production requires on the part of both managers and workers the virtues of patience (delayed gratification), sacrifice (a real limiting of one's personal needs to make the process work), corporate loyalty and commitment (the closing off of many individual options) and a sense of belonging. Yet for the system to work, the producer must also be a heavy consumer—and a heavy consumer, almost by definition, is one whose needs must be fulfilled immediately, who is proudly self-indulgent (flaunts it), will always opt for a better deal, and believes it is wise to keep all options open whenever possible. Moreover, to be anything but a winner is a good way to lose momentum and "die."

The two poles I describe are obvious caricatures, but there is enough inner conflict in most of us to respond to these polarities. My generation was raised to produce; then, at midlife, we were told by television that we "deserved" to have it all. In some respects the middle-class "mid-life crisis" was a creature of this conflict, and those hard-nosed, productive, dull men who suddenly walked away from their families and their jobs to begin new and more "self-fulfilling" life styles in the sixties were caught up in this conflict of values. Clearly the values of consumption are the values of the humanistic psychologies exploited by the media to sell soap.

The children of my middle-class generation began by hoping that they could have it all from the beginning, but soon found out this was not to be and so became the hardest working generation of young professionals and managers in history. But to a surprising extent their goal is not production but consumption, or, as they have written on T-shirts at the Harvard Business School, "The one with the most toys when he dies, wins."

This change of values from production to consumption, and the conflict it entails, has raised problems for management. Many models have been tried with mixed and sometimes little success, most of them based on one psychological theory or another and usually having to do with motivation.

In recent years the model of low-profile management and maximum participation in decisions, with an emphasis on crisis management, has given way somewhat to the model of the manager as coach. The coach model is a warm, articulate, decisive parent figure who leads with a kind of charismatic or inspirational style. This suggests that business and industry have come to realize that a manager, whatever the personal style, is always *in loco parentis*. In this time of a rather sketchily parented work force, a strong and decisive parent who looks after employees, registering concern for their performance while setting clear goals for them, gets the best results.

In terms of therapeutic theory, more emphasis is being put on a powerful positive transference as a means of accomplishing a task, although the Skinnerian carrot and stick always lurks in the simple fact that workers are paid on the basis of performance and general merit.

How do these insights make themselves felt in the world of the parish minister? Parish ministers, although often functioning as managers, are dealing mainly with volunteers rather than a paid work force. To the extent that they see their job as accomplishing discrete tasks, clergy have never had the hard tools of money, promotions, demotions and firing to condition the performance of church workers. Indeed, whatever the parish minister's style, he or she has always had to depend on the good will of the parishioners to get anything done that the sexton, parish secretary or choir director didn't do. The situation is further complicated by the fact that ministers are paid by the very workers to whom they are delegating routine parish tasks.

All this is to say that the administration of a parish is vastly different from the management of business and industry, on the one hand, as well as from the job of a paid hospital or museum director of volunteers, whose salary is paid by the hospital or museum, not the volunteers. Nevertheless parish ministers are *in loco parentis* and so must make a decision, based on how they assess their own parental talent, as to what kind of parent to be. Neither in the family nor in parish administration is the parental role set in stone; in fact, except in the memories of older ministers and parishioners, there are few specifically male and female jobs, but a behavioral range of choices that extends from strict and assertive to permissive and "enabling."

The choices we make on this spectrum will be influenced by our beliefs about human motivation. What enables Christians to join in a voluntary corporate endeavor and maintain high morale? This is the empirical way of looking at things, the question of administration set as a problem to be solved. The classical theological answer is conversion to Jesus Christ as Lord and Savior. I would contend that any empirical answer that ignores or subordinates the theological answer, although it may "work" very well, is not what our vocation is about.

In some mysterious way, more or less, to a greater or lesser extent, from time to time and with ups and downs, people join to form a parish church because they believe or hope or suspect or wish that they have been saved from sin and death by God in the person of Jesus Christ. Of all the tasks for which a parish minister is responsible, it is the work of administration that is most likely to get separated from the real purpose of the parish. It can become a nightmarish, boring burden, or it can become a fascinating field of expertise enjoyed for its own sake, or it can become the place where a minister wins and keeps power—again, for its own sake. The key to keeping the work of administration from taking on a boring or seductive life of its own is to understand it as a mode of service, to see its diaconal dimensions. Viewing administration as a vocation to serving others does have its hazards, however; it may rapidly become a way to get and keep power over others. Parish administration should serve the worship of God. The worship of God is the central purpose of the parish and what distinctively Christian community there will be, will derive from this purpose.

Much of what may go on in a parish will have nothing to do with worship, or else the minister and congregation will not remember how it is related to worship. The reason someone should be elected to a vestry or board of deacons, for example, is to maintain a place where God is to be worshipped, not to honor a hardworking lay person or maintain a winning parish image in the community or provide some local entrepreneur an arena where he or she can catch the eye of other, more powerful, entrepreneurs.

The reason one raises money is primarily to maintain a place and a program around the worship of God. A parish does not raise money to look good, to show that it can do it, to "go over the top," to exceed last year's canvas goals, or to mount an adversary campaign of canvassers against the canvassed.

Now, neither of these tasks — choosing a member of the vestry or raising money — is defined canonically as the function of the parish minister in the Episcopal Church. A governing board elects its own or sets up the process for a parish-wide election. Yet any parish minister who stays out of this process completely, who makes no attempt to make it a matter of theological significance through the use of vestry retreats or providing a serious running commentary on the process, is not doing enough. The same is equally true of fundraising or any kind of canvassing. How money is raised and spent in a parish makes a powerful theological statement.

The reason for keeping parish records is to facilitate communications within the parish, particularly communications having to do with corporate worship and the community that derives from it. Records are not kept to show off one's computer by sending out a daily shower of form letters, congratulating parishioners on their birthdays or wedding anniversaries, or the baptismal anniversaries of their children. Adult education is done to give added depth and seriousness to worship, not to teach the wonders of space technology or the art of macrame or physical fitness.

I say all of these obvious things mainly to make the point that the beginning of good motivation for lay members of a parish—and its clergy as well—is to make sure that what people are asked to do makes sense in terms of what the parish is *for*. The best possible motivation depends on good orientation within a meaningful context, the assurance that one is making a significant contribution to a purposeful enterprise. Busy work, or even necessary work that is perceived as unrelated to any clear purpose, is the enemy of happy administration. It is also the enemy of self-esteem.

What this means is that the greatest possible parish participation is not necessarily a good thing in itself, especially if half of the participation is actually irrelevant to the purpose of the parish. Needless committees and commissions whose main purpose is to "create community" do not create community at all, but hostility and resistance. Community for its own sake tends to generate busy work, since most Americans tend to feel guilty sitting around talking with no task to perform. However this does not mean that the work necessary to maintain a worshipping community is to be organized so efficiently that no one needs to know anyone else to get it done.

It is often said that men like work as a field of achievement while women like work as a place of community. When men are laid off they miss the job; when women are laid off, they miss the people. These stereotypes are silly but, like many other stereotypes, they can be helpful, too. The parish may be the only institution in American life which contains both sexes, yet has its customary work patterns established by women. The work of the church has certainly — in this century, in the United States — been women's territory, which means that all work in a parish, whether it is purposeful or just busy, tends to be for the purpose of community building. This is as true for the men involved as it is for women. Where the work does not serve the ends of the parish, the community can become cliquish and exclusive. Of course any working group *can* turn cliquish and exclusive, but this exclusivity is more likely to happen when the work is not related clearly to the purposes of the whole community.

As I said of preaching, a secondary but important consideration in administration is self-regard. A parish administrator who understands this will, slowly, along with preaching, education, and personal example, construct a world in which it is acceptable to do things badly, a world where a kind of specialized efficiency is not valued highly, a world where excellent performance is not as important as intention and adequacy.

What keeps people from doing a job adequately? One, they don't see the point of the job. Two, they have a bad self-image. Three, they are afraid of failure or of making a fool of themselves. The double purpose of task groups, getting the task done (someday, somehow) while building community (mainly talking to one another about the important things of life and keeping communication and gossip flowing) does put the efficiency and performance dimension of parish functioning into proper perspective. It is important, however, that the parish function adequately, that ministers and parishioners do what they say they are going to do, and that attention is paid to the real value of human time in a society where people are working very hard just to pay the rent, care for children or elderly parents, or to maintain the barest framework of a social and community life.

I agree with Bruce Reed, the English psychologist of religion, that community which is not directly related to the worship of God, but nevertheless derives from what one might call the model household of the Eucharist, should be built in the world, not in the parish. Yet in the United States that is not quite right. Again and again, granted the transiency and carelessness for human beings endemic in American society, the parish simply has to provide some initial, substitute community. Yet a part of the minister's job is to enable parishioners to free themselves from dependency on the parish as a global exclusive community that meets all the social needs of the congregation.

One means of motivation that I think is little understood in parish administration is the place of praise. Certainly the public recognition at parish-wide occasions is regarded as essential by most administrators. "If you don't do it," they tell you, "you're dead." In most parishes people are recognized "for all the work they did" or "for all the time they gave." The recognition will be given usually by the rector, or perhaps by the senior warden. For the most part recognition is given to roughly the same lay persons year after year, as these lay persons carry the burden and heat of the years (not the day). Time and work put into parish maintenance, as well as even sheer busyness, are emphasized at each parish-wide occasion as the marks of distinction (or perhaps salvation) in the parish. It is underlined that the recognition is earned, and ministers learn quickly that those who get it believe they deserve it. They got it the old-fashioned way: they earned it. It should be added that these people often control the vineyard in which they labor; they are power figures and not about to make room for new laborers in the vineyard. Evangelical they aren't. These may be good, kind, helpful people, but in a curious way they control the recognition in the parish. Those who slave away in the vineyard (and the work is often presented as hard and unpleasant) get the praise.

The message is salvation by works, and new people in the parish quickly learn that their acceptance is conditional. They may be indefatigable workers themselves and eager to get involved in parish affairs, but this involvement and acceptance turns out to be harder than it looks. The parish double-binds them. It tells them that their salvation depends on good works and then makes it clear that good works are for those who have earned the right to do them—the faithful old-timers.

It is important to make a distinction between praise and recognition here. Praise is lacking in precision and it fails to define in any detail what is to be praised. "That's great!" "Tonight I want to express our gratitude to one of our great parishioners!" "You're fantastic"—or incredible, or great, or fabulous. Praise goes only one way, permits no feedback, is unilateral, and quite literally creates ambivalence in its recipients. When we are fulsomely praised, we begin to feel uncomfortable; inside our heads, we start to ask rude questions.

"Who does this turkey think he is to praise me? What am I supposed to do? Blush and stammer and disagree? What is he after?"

Vague and undefined praise actually succeeds in distancing the one praising from the one praised. "I applaud the stand that you are taking!" "Great. Thanks a lot. Here I am on a stage acting—there you are in the audience applauding. Is there any commitment here?"

Recognition is different. It is most effective when it is concrete and specific, and voiced at the time rather than at some public occasion. "You know, what you said about the exclusion of newcomers at the sermon feedback session last Sunday was really helpful. It needed to be said, and it had to be said by an old-timer." Or, "The sexton told me you were down here with a shovel to get that snow off the front walk of the church before the eight o'clock communion on Wednesday. I really appreciate your having done that."

Or, "I liked the way you saw that Bill had something on his mind and got it out of him at the vestry meeting Monday. It really helped move the whole meeting along."

If one intends to give public recognition to people, even at the parish annual meeting, it should be for specific behavior.

"I want to call to the congregation's attention that Alice Jones put a lot of effort and imagination and time this year into entirely restructuring the budget so that even I can understand it. The point of presenting the budget this way is to make clear what our priorities are. We're grateful to

you, Alice, for helping us to see ourselves more clearly as
a parish in terms of what we think is important."

What recognition of this sort does is to take something
someone has done and fit it into the overall pattern of
meaning that structures parish life. At its best, recognition
is a form of teaching, even theological teaching. Since it
usually comes from the rector, recognition is, of course, to
some degree a form of hierarchical reward. People are
creaturely; they like that. Yet the deeper motivation
tapped is the need for significance and purposefulness.
The deeper reaction is not, "The rector likes me," but
"What I do at church makes sense out of my life."

Assuming that the purpose of administration is clearly to
serve God by maintaining a place and a community for
divine worship, what kind of leadership is most
appropriate for this purpose? Here again the dynamic of
transference-countertransference is important. I said
earlier that there was a wide range of choices between
strict and permissive, but the notion of these two polar
opposites is reductionist in itself. Different leadership
styles may be adapted to meet different situations in the
same long-term ministry to a single parish. In ministry,
consistency of purpose is as important as consistency of
style.

With this in mind, it is important to think about how
God administers the world, or how he was perceived to
have administered the world in the Bible. After God made
the world, he got so discouraged with it that he almost
destroyed it. Then God chose a rich Aramean and sent
him out to start a church in the middle of nowhere, a
church made up mainly of his own family and their slaves
and other hangers-on. From then on God for the most part

turned over the administration to patriarchs, male rulers who were not much into mutual ministry, who did not ask for feedback, but used to get it from God via the prophets. Let's face it. God couldn't administer his way out of a wet paper bag, and when he tried to do it in person, in the flesh, he got crucified. God's communications skills were terrible, his administrative style was inconsistent and usually authoritarian, and his achievements and successes were few. As the late skipper of the Challenger space shuttle said in a television interview, "Sitting up there in space is a little bit like being God. You look down and you can actually see the drought areas grow. You can see the cities. You see great empty land masses. And you say to yourself, 'There aren't too many humans down there. The whole planet is just hopelessly mismanaged.'"

You can either say that administration is not God's strong suit, or else you can say that God's administration is not our administration. From the Bible one would gather that God emphasizes certain dimensions of administration over others. God pays close attention. God cares about what happens, how things turn out. God intervenes, but seldom from a position of authority or power. Certainly by the time of Isaiah, the Hebrew prophets had the power and authority of tradition, yet, as Jesus said, the great prophets were ridiculed, humiliated, even stoned. The metaphor of God as a brooding hen wishing to take Jerusalem under her wings doesn't sound much like a modern manager, or an enabler trying to let people discover their autonomous selves. Jerusalem chose not to go under those brooding wings, but to save herself by her own power and cunning. God's administration depends on the revealed assurance of ultimate safety in the life, teaching, suffering, death and resurrection, of

Jesus Christ. It depends on our assurance of our own value in the eyes of God, our assurance that we were not born by mistake and forced to live to no purpose beyond the survival of the self, our assurance of God's attention and care for us in this life through the Holy Spirit.

Now an ordained minister is not God, but the administration of a parish should be aimed at the construction of a parish world that reflects these aspects of God's concern for the world itself. Ultimate safety, salvation, the assurance that everything will be, as we say to children, "all right" in the end, is a very different thing from a fantasy of safety that we have come to as part of our calculated defense against reality. Neither does such assurance depend, as therapists seem to think, on a secure first year of infancy. It does not save us from the normal fears and anxieties of existence, rather, it gives us some reason to deal with these fears and anxieties in a way that is less destructive to ourselves and others, a way to love and seek justice in spite of our initial fears and anxieties.

This is why the worship of God, particularly the Eucharist, is the primary, central purpose of ordained parish ministry. It is a symbolic acting out of the dynamic of this ultimate safety, the dynamic of salvation.

What does this mean for parish administration? It means that the mounting of this worship must be careful and reverent. To carry the message of salvation adequately, the service must be free of needless or irrelevant surprise. Lay readers should be trained and present and ready, and they should understand the significance of what they read.

The relationship between the ordained minister and the organist/choir-director should be given as much time as necessary to make it a collaborative one. Few things are so destructive to the structure of ultimate safety in worship as a war between the minister and the organist, unless it is a war between a parish minister and an assistant minister.

The administrative task behind mounting Sunday worship involves more than telling acolytes, ushers, altar guilders and choir members that *prima donna* attention-getting behavior is not appropriate in worship. Instead, it involves a growing assurance on the part of these participants that they have the attention of the rector, and beyond that, the attention of God. The serious administrator does not regard time spent with any active participants in worship as time wasted.

Indeed, attention is an important part of all parish administration, and this is not a simple thing to learn and practice. The trouble is that attention to individuals is hard to maintain—perhaps, at times, impossible to maintain—when one is concerned with accomplishing a task. The people involved tend to become simply obstructions or facilitators, useful or not useful.

In the past, this double bind was overcome by parish calling. Home visits provided a time for giving a different kind of attention to the person. Today the number of empty homes in some parishes bring this time-honored custom into question.

I have noticed that there are parish ministers who do seem to have developed a kind of timing. It is similar to the timing of a sophisticated group leader who, seeing it is time to let up on a task, starts paying attention instead to the maintenance of group relationships and process. In the conversations that surround such tasks as recruitment, calling up people to find a church school superintendent, or a head of the every member canvas, or someone for the altar guild, the pastor will suddenly ease up, begin asking the person what she thinks about the task, from there to discussing how things are going.

These moments of letting up are very like prayer. In a sense, prayer is any time we forget about issues of maintenance and survival and time as a non-renewable resource, and instead give our full attention to the circumstances of the moment.

Perhaps one example is in order here. I once agreed to meet someone for lunch in the foyer of an inner-city cathedral. I was sitting in a chair in the shadows waiting when two members of the cathedral staff, both male priests in their early thirties, came trotting down the stairs talking and joking with one another in an animated fashion. They were both handsome and athletic jogging types, tanned and fit, beautifully dressed in expensive clothes.

Suddenly a girl of twelve or thirteen years old came through the door and stood looking lost and disoriented. One of the priests walked over to her and asked, "Is there something I could do to help you?"

The girl was dirty. Her face was dirty, her hair was filthy, her clothes were torn. She said something to the priest, but because she apparently had a speech impediment, it was impossible to make out what she said. The priest, who was tall, bent over and looked her in the eye and said, "I couldn't make out what you said."

She tried again. This time the priest tried to interpret the noises. "You want to see Father. . . . I couldn't get the name, at some kind of center?"

When she tried again, the priest came as close as he could to mimicking the sounds coming out of her to see if something would click in his memory. "Father Joe at the Chessie Howdie Center."

This time she began to laugh and he began to laugh. Suddenly she said, clear as a bell, "I want to see Father Jones at the Chelsea Housing Center."

"Oh," he said, "Father Jones!" And they both laughed again. "He's got a little room way up on the fourth floor of the parish house. I'd better go up with you." And he took her hand and off they went.

While this transaction was taking place, the child underwent a kind of transformation. Her posture changed, her face went from expressionless to animated, and finally enough fear was driven out to free her second language, her school language, so that she could speak English rather than underclass Chelsea. The person who finally responded seemed to be a different person from the one who asked the initial question.

Now those two priests were probably going out to a working lunch. The transaction with the girl took at least twenty minutes, perhaps more, a lot of lunch time. But from the careful, patient listening of the priest, what the child got was attention, almost sacramental attention. A statement was made. "What this child has to say deserves attention. Everything will now stop until what she has to say is heard."

It is not merely attention for the powerless and needy that is required. Most people live without much attention being paid to them apart from their usefulness to someone. The point is not that parish ministers should pay attention to everyone in the parish; it is rather that they should model attention-paying behavior and point out the connection between such behavior and prayer at every opportunity, including spiritual direction and classes on Christian spirituality. People become aware of what ultimate safety means in an environment where paying attention has a high priority and where it is clear that they are being attended to.

In sum, it seems to me that the assumptions of counseling theory need close, discriminating examination in the administration of a parish. Recognition is not the same thing as "strokes." It has a cognitive aspect related to structural purposefulness, as well as serving as a psychological reward. It is a form of deep Christian education.

Building community into the parish world simply to provide psychological support, where the community is unrelated to the overall purpose of the parish, is not the same as discovering community in the process of serving the true purpose of the parish. People need to know that what they are doing makes a kind of theological sense; it motivates them as much as concrete rewards designed to give pleasure to the ego.

Efficiency carried to a level of ball-bearing perfection makes for an exclusive church, where people can avoid any serious encounter with one another. Yet adequacy of performance and faithfulness in getting the work of the parish done is essential to the self-esteem of Christians.

At the heart of parish administration is the construction of a world where mortal fears and worldly anxieties are never used to force participation, where no parishioner is afraid of making a fool of herself, where no one needs to worry about whether he "looks good," where failure is never regarded as definitive and winning is restricted to parish softball games. This will not be accomplished well. If it is accomplished barely or at all, it will be because it is done for the glory of a God who loves us and whom we come together to worship.

Liturgy

Different people experience worship differently, and it is my opinion that people who write about liturgy on any level should make their perceptual bias clear early on. My own ideas about worship are idiosyncratic, and there is a reason for it. As a child I was myopic, but managed to conceal it through the fourth grade by peering at things in the distance through a hole I made by partially clenching one fist. This rather restricted the range of what I could see. As a result I became more than a little dependent on my ears and my nose and, in a curious way, on my nearsighted observation of discrete objects. My eyes have a tendency to focus and my mind to translate the image immediately into an abstract idea about it. If I give my visual attention to a service of the Eucharist, for example, I will notice mistakes; if there are no mistakes, I will note that it has been done perfectly. If the vestments are beautiful and the choreography elegant, I will note that, too. Yet I experience these thoughts as distractions.

If, on the other hand, the service—particularly the lessons from Scripture—is read intelligently, clearly, and expressively and the music is pleasing, I shall be aware of that only in retrospect. On a good day, my whole attention will be on the holy narrative in which I am participating. All this is to say that the visual does not make immediate sense for me, but rather requires that I make sense out of it, that I translate it into thoughts. Spoken language and music, by contrast, bring forth from me a more spontaneous and whole response. There was a time when it distracted me to hear the service read as if it were the directions from the back of a soup can, or, for that matter, as if it were the last act of King Lear, but perhaps because the language is so familiar to me now such eccentricities no longer bother me. As long as I can hear what is read, I am content and can worship without distraction.

Liturgical music is a somewhat more complicated matter for me. I am a musical person. I like to sing and play the piano by ear. I am not a musical snob; I enjoy singing the grand old Victorian howlers in the hymnal as much as the next person. But I am more of a performance snob than I would like to be. My experience of worship is vulnerable to music that is off key or off tempo, to instruments badly played, to choirs or solo voices singing inappropriate music badly. There are hymns, still, even in the new hymnal of the Episcopal Church, where the theology is too bad to be ignored ("Gaze we on his glorious scars") and it can destroy a Sunday morning for me.

As for the kinetic aspects of worship, I am of two minds. When I celebrate the Eucharist, I am rather like W.C. Fields: if there is a wastebasket within six feet of me, I will step in it. For this reason I like to keep ceremony and movement to a minimum. When engaged in any kind of elaborately choreographed liturgy, I find myself worrying more than worshipping. As a member of the congregation I am happy with what seems to me the natural movement of sitting and standing and kneeling, and I find going from my seat to the altar to receive the bread and wine a particularly significant part of the Eucharist. For Quakers, who regard stillness punctuated by moments of inspiration as the essence of worship, all this movement must seem like so much distracting busy-work.

There is always a temptation for liturgists to justify their perceptual bias with biblical or theological or historical material. Yet a still riskier temptation for liturgists, particularly if they are parish ministers, is to use liturgy as a form of engineering. They are tempted to see it as a way of bringing about social change, or a means of changing the behavior patterns of their particular parish. Liturgy can be used to shore up and support their understanding of "community," even though it is an understanding more often based on therapeutic than biblical or theological assumptions. In all these cases, liturgy is perceived as a tool that can be used to alter human behavior.

In what follows I will attempt to examine this phenomenon, to trace its beginings in the liturgical experimentation of the forties and fifties, and then to speculate on its consequences as they affect the building of a moral world.

The liturgical renewal movement of the forties and fifties was the result of careful historical research. This in itself tended to make it seem somewhat precious and esoteric not only to most American congregations, but to many ordained ministers as well. Americans are seldom persuaded to any kind of change by historical argument. Liturgical change is always slow, difficult and painful. Since ordained ministers are almost always the liturgical experts of any congregation, it is they who must persuade the congregation—first, to see any significant need for liturgical change, then to teach members of the congregation some basic liturgical rationale, and then to lead them in implementing the actual changes. This is not a simple thing to do. What it amounts to is taking something that has always been regarded as the ordained minister's business and making it the business of the laity.

For Episcopalians this was particularly difficult, for as it was spelled out in canon law, liturgical decisions really belonged to the priest. However if priests simply invoked the power of canon law in order to try and change the liturgy, they were asking not only for trouble, but for runaway rebellion on the part of the congregation — or else a steady exodus of parishioners to the nearest parish church where the rector had no such harebrained ideas.

Before the first trial editions of the prayer book in the sixties, the major changes in the Episcopal Church's liturgy were part of a larger movement that involved not only radical changes in Christian education, but in many cases the building of new churches as well. The fifties were a time of growth in many denominations; parishes discovered that their buildings were inadequate, and many worship spaces were redesigned. Liturgy and church architecture cannot — or should not — be separated. Since the heart of the new liturgy was a eucharist understood as a family meal, with the priest as *pater* or *mater familias* standing behind the altar and facing the congregation, new churches designed for this new liturgy were as unfamiliar to the eyes of the congregation as the liturgy itself.

The pews of the congregation were often placed around the altar in a semi-circle. A commitment to this unfamiliar structure was a commitment to the new liturgy as well. For this reason, wiser pastors would prepare people for the new building by first preparing them for the new liturgy. Those congregations who became convinced that the new liturgy was important and necessary were also the most enthusiastic about a new building. It should be added here that the shape of this liturgy and its architectural context were understood theologically, to the extent that there was a single theological rationale for it, as representing the *oikos*, the household of the coming great church. The liturgical renewal movement, although begun within European Catholicism, soon became an ecumenical endeavor, albeit unofficially, and began to include liturgists from every branch of main line Protestantism, particularly Anglicans and Lutherans. The participants in the "family meal" as it was originally construed was not the nuclear family, but the *oikumene*, the "household of the known world," a powerful theological construct of the early church.

There was, then, a package of changes—in Christian education, in liturgy, and in church architecture—which the more conscientious of the clergy felt obliged to effect during that period. At the same time it became quickly apparent that no significant change could be made without considerable resistance on the part of their parishioners. As a result of this resistance a curious thing happened: the issue of change itself became more important to many clergy than the actual changes they were seeking. Suddenly clergy began to perceive themselves as "change agents" and to become concerned with techniques for effecting change. This interest in the change process itself provided an opening for therapeutic theory to insinuate itself into the matter of liturgy, for better or worse.

One assumption of counseling theory is that resistance within the counseling situation is largely unconscious and often unrelated to the actual reasons the client gives for resisting. In counseling this tends to lead to a kind of distrust of words as simple purveyors of information. Counselors are taught to "attend," to be aware of the context within which the words are uttered. The counselor puts the words in the context of past sessions, observes the client's body language, even examines the syntax of the utterance for indications of passivity or aggression.

The reasons put forward for certain behaviors may, by the logic of counseling, have little to do with the behaviors themselves. There may be "deeper" (by which the counselor means unconscious) reasons for these behaviors. In the counseling situation, where a client bedeviled by self-defeating behaviors and consequent low self-esteem comes to a counselor with the express purpose of being freed of these behaviors, this logic is appropriate and clinically helpful. Where it is applied to the corporate life of a parish, however, the same logic can create a general ambience of mutual mistrust.

For it is impossible to live in community where people cannot trust spoken language. To take one example, if I say to the rector or to a canvasser, "I don't want to pledge any money for the new church because I really hate the architecture," I may find it a bit Kafka-esque if he or she *hears* me say, "I don't want to pledge any money to the new church because I don't feel included in the parish community." It will be even more confusing for me if shortly thereafter I am asked to serve on the new building committee or some minor subdivision thereof. Even if I accept the offer, I am more likely to feel pressured than included. I know when I'm being manipulated. What are these people after, anyway? Probably my money.

In this strange twilight world of metacommunication, where "no" in different contexts can mean "maybe" or even "yes," where the listener always knows better than the speaker what the speaker intends, one begins to experience a pervasive sense of unreality. Metacommunication itself is a very inexact mode of communication. Technically, it is that part of communication concerned with letting my listener know how the content of my communication is to be used or interpreted. If I say something to you and wink, I am telling you one thing; if I use the same words while nodding earnestly, it is something else entirely. In the second, I am emphasizing their seriousness. Or I may begin a sentence "Now you may find this incredible..." or "Trust me..." or "You may not like what I have to say...," any one of which is simply a verbalized metacommunication, telling the listener how the information to follow is to be interpreted.

Yet there are contexts within contexts. A wink, from anyone, is a fairly precise piece of communication, but "Trust me..." from a used car salesman does not communicate the same thing as "Trust me..." from a brain surgeon. Even the nodding of my head can be interpreted to mean earnestness, pure and simple, or something as complex as "I am a New Age person." In the past, most people learned to handle these cues without thinking much about them. They served to give shades of meaning to blunt statements. Where society was more or less stable, there grew up a shared repertoire of such cues. We could use them without much conscious effort and yet trust in the fact that our meaning would not be grossly misinterpreted.

Metacommunication as a learned skill is a pure product of therapeutic culture. It has become an integral part of television advertising, management training, public relations, and even the formulation of public policy. It is at the heart of political campaigning. It has made a major contribution to the degradation of spoken and written language and the untrustworthiness of verbal communication which has become endemic in our culture.

If an example is needed here, I think of the celebrated statement that George Bush made to a labor union leader after he had debated Geraldine Ferraro during the 1984 presidential campaign.. "I kicked a little ass last night!" said Bush. Presumably, he was not so much claiming victory in the debate as trying to say, "Trust me. I'm a tough guy like you." I suspect that that message was not what the labor union leader heard; it may not even have been what Bush intended that he hear. Only one thing is clear. His statement was disturbing, confusing, and imprecise—a metaphor gone completely berserk. This often happens when we try to address what we perceive to be the unconscious of other people, or attempt to engage their fantasies rather than their conscious, intentional cognition. It is not that this can't be done, but that it can't be done precisely and with predictable results.

Along the same lines, part of the Reagan administration's rationale for bombing Tripoli in 1986 was the notion that if the bombs killed Khadaffi's wife, or some of his children, this would discredit Khadaffi as a leader because Bedouins don't trust leaders who can't protect their families. The bombing was to be a message, a communication to the Libyan people, that their leader was not trustworthy. Whatever the bombing communicated to the Libyan people, it communicated to our European allies that our own leader was not trustworthy, and it communicated to the American people that it was no longer safe to travel in Europe. The bombing of Tripoli accomplished, by a single act, more damage to the United States and Europe than all the Arab terrorism up to that point. So much for the precision of metacommunication.

The notion that we can consciously manipulate and shape the context which will receive and interpret the words we speak or write assigns great importance to that context. Jeffrey Masson, in his book attacking the integrity of Freud's work (*The Assault on Truth: Freud's Suppression of the Seduction Theory)*, makes an important point. He accuses Freud of altering his theory that hysteria in women was caused by childhood seduction at the hands of adults who were *in loco parentis*, and stated instead that hysteria was caused by mere fantasies of seduction. Masson claims that Freud did this to avoid the opprobrium his original theory had generated among his colleagues and the general public. If Masson is right, then by doing so Freud helped to begin the erosion of the distinction between fantasy and reality which has become a communicational plague for our time. Our growing distrust of language as a mode of negotiating with reality, instead of whatever interpretation of events serves those established in power, has brought us close to believing, as recent presidential elections might suggest, that the most pleasant fantasies will win and simply become our reality until some more pleasant fantasy is presented to us.

It was into a church infected with this growing distrust of the spoken and written word that liturgical renewal came. Although such renewal was solidly based on historical research and motivated by a desire for authentic liturgical forms, many parish ministers began to justify it to themselves and to each other on socio-psychological grounds. Liturgy, by this view, was a powerful form of symbolic language. It communicated at a less than conscious level some very profound truths, which had the power to affect both world-view and behavior. Many parish ministers believed that the church should become less naive about this powerful mode of communication and learn to use it for its own renewal, by which they meant the community life of the parish—the single most important issue in the rapidly growing suburban parishes of the fifties and sixties.

Our model for this community was the family—and, too often, the nuclear family. The new shape of the Eucharist, the priest celebrating face to face with the people, lent itself to confirming this model. The Eucharist was not some mystical exercise on the part of an anonymous priest aimed at some distant transcendent God in the east, praying for a congregation infantilized to a foetal position in their pews; it was a family meal. The priest as symbolic parent stood behind the altar facing the gathered family, who, in the best of all possible worlds, would be standing in a semi-circle and able to see each other's faces, unable to avoid the intimacy of a family meal. God was not hidden somewhere off beyond the east wall of the church, but present in the midst of them.

This was incarnational worship at its most intimate, and many clergy firmly believed that it would revolutionize the quality of relationships within the parish. To a greater degree than we understood at the time, the emphasis had moved slightly away from the simple, direct worshipping of God toward the work of bringing about attitudinal change in the congregation. Some clergy, and some more than others, were beginning to engage in a bit of psychosocial engineering.

In one sense we were also beginning to think of liturgy as a more trustworthy mode of communication than simple spoken or written language. Liturgy seemed to control and shape the context within which the message would be received and interpreted. Unfortunately, along with this assumption went its corollary: the message was aimed as much at the congregation as it was at God. Certainly in true worship we trust our inwardness to the words and movement of the liturgy to renew and reorder it as an offering to God. For us to do this, to give up what we like to think of as our autonomy and let our inwardness be shaped by a power outside ourselves, is to engage in an act of consummate trust.

In former times, the reason for our trust lay in our belief that the definition of the human and the divine and their interaction in the Eucharist was the product of the historical wisdom of the church, not the product of a liturgical committee. Historical continuity has always been regarded as part of the environment of safety essential to true worship. To believe that one has been saved is to believe that one is ultimately safe. From the perspective of salvation, a church building is a sacramental expression of ultimate safety. The medieval concept of sanctuary, retrieved from history so powerfully in recent times to provide a safe space for Central American refugees from tyranny, can also be seen as a metaphor for the safety of our own undefended and vulnerable inwardness in liturgical worship.

Those scholars of the Episcopal Church who revised the Book of Common Prayer had a profound understanding of all this. They took enormous care in maintaining or even reestablishing historical continuity in their revision. Yet it is important to note that even with all this attention to continuity and tradition, any form of liturgical change is bound to cause resistance. To the credit of these serious and disciplined liturgical scholars, they never trivialized this resistance to the level of psychobabble about "fear of change." They understood the spiritual seriousness of the resistance, and proceeded slowly, patiently, prayerfully, and with honest good will to educate the church, clergy and laity, in history and theology.

Where liturgical change went wrong, to the extent that it did go wrong, it was in those cases where therapeutic theory began to replace historical research and theological reflection as a justification for the change. Where change generated spiritual pain and extreme cognitive dissonance, resulting in resistance among members of a congregation, the resistance deserved better treatment than it got. In many cases this resistance was dismissed as psychological "rigidity"; it was to be gotten around by "strategies," which addressed the resistance as a form of pathology. Merely the choice of the word "strategy" suggests an adversary relationship between priest and congregation that added to the pain and confusion.

As the sixties progressed and prayer books for trial use began to appear, some parish priests, supported by as many members of their congregations as could be persuaded to become interested in matters liturgical, began a period of experimentation. In some cases it followed upon serious historical and theological study, with careful preparation of the whole congregation for the experiments to come. In other parishes, particularly those where a deep involvement in new forms of adult education had created core groups of parishioners much influenced by the human potential movement, it took a very different form. There experimentation was based less on theology and more on certain psychological assumptions about what it was to be "fully human." To be fully human was to be spontaneous, joyful, autonomous, unafraid of intimacy, eager to touch others and look into their eyes, not hung up on authority, undismayed by disorder—that matrix of creativity—and above all, glowing with self-esteem. It is hard to gauge the extent of this experimentation, which ranged from an occasional balloon all the way to mime, slide shows, rock bands and fifteen minutes of the kiss of peace.

Although these liturgical experiments brought about a degree of euphoria in some parishes, such euphoria was fragile and often downright fraudulent. There was a message in the air: if you were not filled with delight by all this carrying on, you were not, perhaps, quite living up to your full human potential. To put it another way, those parishioners who were uncomfortable with such worship found themselves with "bad" feelings in a situation where feeling good was supposed to be the measure of one's full humanity. Yet all of this on the surface seems harmless enough. Adult Christians, one would imagine, should have been able to take the situation in stride or leave it alone, praying to themselves, "This, too, shall pass. . . ."

However, there was one aspect of this liturgical experimentation that was not only far from harmless, but a radical departure from a basic rule of liturgical worship. Good liturgy never tells us how to feel; feeling is not an area of human freedom. We can choose either to feel or not to feel, but we cannot choose what to feel. I know of no place either in the 1928 or present Prayer Book where we are told to be grateful, joyful, or penitent. These are all cognitive-emotional states that are given to us by the grace of God. There are no prayers in the Prayer Book which begin, "We come before you this morning, O God, with grateful hearts," or "O God, our hearts are full of joy at this Easter season," or "Accept our heart-felt penitence on this Ash Wednesday." Instead, we ask God to give us grateful or joyful or penitent hearts, knowing that we cannot conjure up feelings on demand.

Even on a psychological level, if we can believe the late Gregory Bateson, it is not helpful to tell someone to "be spontaneous" any more than it is helpful to tell a grieving person to "cheer up" or a child who has just punched a sibling to "be sorry." People who have been raised in families where appropriate feelings were not only expected, but demanded at all times, are often out of touch with their feelings altogether. A basic rule of Christian ethics is that people are responsible only for their conscious decisions, never for unconscious motivations. We feel what we feel. Our freedom lies in our choice of specific behaviors.

Some young ministers who were deeply involved in the civil rights movement, and later in the movement to end the war in Vietnam, believed that liturgy could be used to engineer attitudes towards racism and war. There was much argument at the time within the movement about whether behavior could be changed by changing attitudes, or whether it was the behavior that had to be changed first and attitudes would follow. The latter argument served as the basis for struggling not only for a civil rights law, but for the use of the national guard to enforce it. These young movement ministers began to experiment with liturgy as a mode of attitudinal and behavioral engineering, with consciousness-raising (as they called it) in regard to such issues as racism and war.

I can remember ecumenical college chaplaincy services where elaborate sound systems attached to tape recorders blasted out a kind of audio-collage of rock music, poetry, newscasts, and random cuts from patriotic speeches. Slide and movie projectors flashed gruesome images of war or racial oppression onto a screen over the altar. In parish eucharists I saw the use of chancel drama, dance, or mime to project harsh, bruising messages about various social evils in a way that was meant to "penetrate the defenses" of the congregation. In this sort of liturgy racism was not presented as a form of discriminatory and unjust behavior, but as a kind of evil unconscious fear deep in the hearts of the congregation. War was seldom examined rationally or placed in any kind of historical context. It was presented on the psychological level of aggression, something that had to be raised to consciousness and rooted out of the human heart for good if the human race was to survive. Racism and war were seen as problems, and liturgy was seen as a solution. Racism and war were seen as sickness, and liturgy was seen as therapy. The extreme forms of this sort of liturgy were rare and largely restricted to college campuses, but an essentially therapeutic rationale for this or that liturgical innovation was not uncommon in many parts of the church. Too often such liturgical innovation was concerned with telling the congregation how they were feeling, or how they ought to be feeling, through various metacommunicational devices or through prayers that were thinly disguised lectures to the congregation.

It is important to note that these tendencies did not amount to a sinister liturgical conspiracy, whereby an energetic cell of liturgists planned a takeover of the church's ceremonies. Therapeutic theory and liturgical experimentation happened to appear on the scene simultaneously. As I have remarked in earlier chapters, the assumptions of therapeutic practice were held by a great many ministers and other professional people by the middle of the sixties. In a similar way, that is how a fair number of ministers thought about liturgy; it is also the way a fair number of Juvenile Court judges thought about sentencing. Liturgy as a form of therapy, or of consciousness-raising, or social engineering, did not last long in the Episcopal Church. It was one part of a period, a brief period, of liturgical experimentation. When the

Book of Common Prayer reached its final form in the seventies and became the church's prayer book, most of the parish priests' energy went into establishing that; resistance on the part of congregations was sufficient to preclude any additional experimentation. When all was said and done, the major innovation to come out of all that experimentation — besides the revised Prayer Book itself — was the notion of the Eucharist as a family meal. The altar was removed from the east wall; the priest stood behind it, facing the congregation.

Just what effect liturgy could have as a consciousness-raising social tool was left in limbo; the experiment was inconclusive and largely dropped. Indeed, some liturgists came to look upon experimental liturgy less as a shaper of the congregation's piety than as an expression of it. If this was the case, then the piety of most congregations must have shifted from various forms of self-expression to a reluctant conformism, along with the consciousness of the nation in general.

Yet the new shape of the Eucharist remained, and with it a question. Was this sense of the Eucharist as a family meal indicative of a shift in the relationship between priest and congregation?

The late Gregory Bateson maintained that there are two basic human relationships, complementary and symmetrical. A complementary relationship is where one person in the relationship is dominant and the other submissive: one a parent, the other a child; one a teacher, the other a disciple; one a boss, the other a worker. By contrast, in a symmetrical relationship two people are related as equals, as is the case with business or tennis partners, or two junior managers at the same level of a corporation. Bateson claimed that both relationships are viable within an orderly social matrix, but that when these relationships begin to deteriorate, they do so in different ways.

In the complementary relationship the dominant becomes more dominant and the submissive more submissive, until the latter is destroyed or else revolts. Bateson used as an example the relationship between an imperial nation and its colonies. In the symmetrical relationship, however, deterioration takes the form of runaway, escalating competition, ending in bloody combat or else a complete split, a "divorce." For this Bateson used as an example the relationship between the Soviet Union and the United States.

The new shape of the Eucharist sacramentally defined the relationship between priest and congregation as symmetrical—eyeball to eyeball. Yet at the same time, paradoxically, it placed the priest *in loco parentis*. In the previous form of the rite, the priest faced in the same direction as the congregation and yet was removed from them, as leader and pioneer. Thus the priest represented the congregation before God. So the relationship between priest and congregation was clearly defined as complementary and hierarchical, as God was defined as transcendent except for the actual moment of communion itself, where the priest turned to the congregation and God became incarnate.

When, instead, the minister faces the people, he or she becomes both parent and partner, indeed, almost parent and adversary in a culture that is as competitive and free of rules as ours. I am reminded of a comment made by Robert Goheen, president of Princeton University during the student turbulence of the late sixties. "The alumni say that they want me to be *in loco parentis*. That's the whole trouble. I *am in loco parentis*. I don't know what to do with them either!" In the very physical shape of the Eucharist, then, the priest becomes an ambiguous figure. When relationships switch from complementary to symmetrical, they are not automatically equipped with a set of rules understood by all. For the rules—indeed, the canons of the church—which regulate the relationship between priest and congregation are designed to maintain a stable complementary relationship, not a symmetrical one. Although new rules may develop in time, the symmetry of the current priest-congregation relationship makes it prone to a runaway escalation of competition (conflict) and, too often, a split (the firing of the rector). This occurs in the absence of any rules or even guidelines for the way this new relationship should best and most coherently be conducted.

When the priest behind the altar faces the congregation, it is assumed that God is to be addressed between the altar and the congregation, or, if the congregation is arranged around the altar, in the midst of the parish family. All eyes should be turned inwards towards the God among us. Yet people still seem to be worshipping a God somewhere beyond the east wall. Their concentration is on the east, but between them and God, and apparently representing God, not them, is the priest. Their concentration is on the celebrant, a distinct person who may be bearded or not, long-haired or crew-cut, gaining weight or surprisingly trim, ugly or beautiful, man or woman, grim or cheerful, sweating or dry, elegantly vested or vested in what appears to be an unmade bed. If his hair is short, is he a preppy? Perhaps a snob? If she's gaining weight, is she pregnant? If she looks trim, is she jogging? Any change in the appearance of the priest has a special significance in this charged atmosphere of transference.

The priest at worship is the same person, ridiculous or sublime, whom one meets in the supermarket, or playing golf, or in a counseling session. The same priest at worship has to a degree lost the theological significance, the sacramental power, to move the transferential consciousness of the congregation beyond the priest leading worship, to God, the center of worship. Even a particularly elegant chasuble or a "creative" stole seems more like *haute couture* than an aesthetic enhancement of worship when it is worn by a priest facing the congregation.

All this is to say that the theological and psychological statement which the implementers of the new shape of liturgy intended to communicate to the congregation may not have been the one that the congregation received. Indeed, the statement received may have been this: the church is an inward-looking community obsessed by the quality of its own interactions and its own survival, with the priest responsible for managing all this acting as a *primus inter pares* but really as a manager without power or a parent of surly adolescent children.

At this point, then, it is hard to say whether the priest represents the congregation before God, or whether the priest represents God before the people. Or is the priest a simple professional, a skilled technician, hired by a congregation to manage conflict and keep a low profile and please as many people as possible at Sunday worship? Are members of the congregation to be regarded as consumers of a liturgical product? This metaphor of consumption is not merely a cynical throwaway on my part. It is a fairly common metaphor for the relationship between priests, their professional skills, and the congregations who pay for them.

I want to emphasize here that I am not making a plea for returning the altar to the east wall and priests to their original place before it. Nor do I believe that doing so would fix everything up and return us to the good old days. Had the rearrangement of things not coincided with the emphasis on the nuclear family as the basis for mental health, the congregation's own response to the change might have been less literal. Then the concept of the *oikos*, the universal family or household, the household of the coming Great Church, the true theological concept that was originally intended, might have prevailed.

If parish ministers take as the proper focus of pastoral care the building of some sort of transitional moral world, they will have to think of the place of liturgy in this project. Or else they will have to think about the place of building such a moral world in the liturgy. The liturgy as a vital, participative narrative that makes ultimate sense out of the human condition is not there to be used. It is not a tool, but a context, and no Christian moral world can be built that does not grow out of eucharistic practice and is not informed with eucharistic significance.

However in the spatial shaping of liturgy, it might be wise to consider that the God revealed to us in Scripture is both transcendent and immanent, and is best and most completely worshipped in both dimensions. As we worship now in most churches, our worship seems to me too exclusively immanental or at least incarnational. The wonder of the Incarnation is the majesty and complex mystery of the one who chose to become incarnate. However much people deny it, fight it, or disclaim it, their deepest fears are about the future of the planet and the total human condition. However hard they try to build safe secondary communities within the chaos of a disintegrating culture, they know the ultimate futility of their task. What is of the planet, indeed, of this world, is not safe. A purely immanental God is less than the God revealed to us in Jesus Christ. The love of God revealed in the Incarnation is not complete without God's universal power to save. We must not be ambiguous in our preaching of the resurrection. God is not the world, but the world's creator, redeemer and sustainer. This is the God we worship, and in whose worship our hope is renewed.

A Makeshift Moral World

For all that has been said about the incursion of therapeutic theory into the moral world of the parish, little has been written about the actual moral code that was affected. By morality, I mean no more than the customary rules for ordering the community and the hardly conscious assumptions that underlay them and from which they derived. Church morality, Christian morality, remained until World War II a model for all responsible corporate behavior in the larger community. Thus the moral world of the parish was the morality of a rural community of manageable size, where continuity, stability, and familiarity made life highly predictable, and it was possible for someone with good judgment and good intentions to be nearly as good as their word.

It was generally agreed, however, that if one moved to the city, this was less likely to happen. People sensed that this morality depended to a degree on being known. Going to the city was putting oneself morally at risk. The man from the city, the city slicker, was less careful about his word (who would know whether he kept it or not? And who would care?). The cities were seen, and to a degree are *still* seen, as centers of sin and immorality as well as centers of great opportunity for energetic individuals.

The social function of Protestantism up until World War II was to reinforce this enlightenment morality with a divine sanction. Sermons were much concerned with matters of sobriety, chastity, honesty in business, hard work, ambition (a good thing), telling the truth, respect for parents, obedience to the law, and other such homely virtues. Most of these virtues became identified with the middle class, since by the early twentieth century their possession practically guaranteed entry to the middle class. Honesty, it was believed, was the best policy, but the word "policy" suggests a sanction for honest behavior more pragmatic than theological.

The middle class is a vague concept in American life and its definition always rather arbitrary. In a predominantly rural and agricultural society, "middle class" is not a useful category; it existed mainly in the industrial and commercial areas. Until World War II being middle class meant owning property, having some savings, working at something commercial or industrial or bureaucratic at a fairly managerial level, and having all the virtues listed above. To be middle class one did not need a college education, but a college education guaranteed secure membership.

Public school teachers were largely women and often second or third generation middle class. They demanded middle-class behavior in the class rooms and taught middle-class values—perhaps with more lasting effect than the preachers did. Thus both church and the public schools were increasingly to make the middle class as accessible as possible to all Americans. Working class kids with good marks and an "A" in deportment went on to finish high school and from there either on scholarship to college or straight to work and within a decade, into the middle class. They knew how to *be* middle class from their church attendance and their public school education.

There was, then, at all times after the industrial revolution real upward mobility in American society. The more complex delineation of an established middle class life increased the distance of the social and economic leap into respectability. In a strange way those who made the leap were required to put themselves together, fabricate themselves like a work of art, or at least a work of the imagination.

This act of fabrication could involve a lot of lying and embroidering about one's origins, and such deceit contributed to the American obsession with hypocrisy— or, as it was later called, "phoniness." A recurring question with American writers of the first quarter of this century had been, what on earth were you supposed to do with yourself if you made money and became a success? Were you doomed to become a pious, middle-class drone? A hard, cold, gimlet-eyed businessman, regular in his church attendance, and harshly judgmental of all who were not as hard-headed and successful as himself? Sinclair Lewis, Sherwood Anderson, Henry James, Willa Cather: all were concerned with authenticity and class. Indeed, the word class itself took on a peculiar meaning in America at that time, going beyond social class to include all those whose position was based entirely on merit— who were not snobs or nobs or, later, phonies. Babe Ruth had class; so did Franklin D. Roosevelt. Someone with "class" had an assimilated morality, a morality of the heart, as opposed to the moral overlay of an upwardly mobile, respectable bourgeois. The literary cliche of the bourgeous social climber was a man who repressed sexuality, generosity, conviviality, artistic sensibility for the single purpose of economic gain and social respectability, and a woman who backed her man all the way. The church was seen by many writers of the time as a part of this social process.

This stereotype, like all stereotypes, amounted to an unfair caricature of middle-class society, but it did raise the issue of upward mobility, an issue which has not gone away in the United States. What do you do when you find yourself suddenly making a great deal more money than you have ever seen before? Who do you become? What do you buy to express what you have become? What new hobbies and interests should you acquire? What new social attitudes towards money and sex and marriage and parenthood and education do you accept? How does your relationship to your working class or lower middle class parents and siblings change? What about your old friends?

This upward mobility was rationalized early on by Spencer's doctrine of the survival of the fittest. Maximizing the potential of the individual at the expense of others improved the gene pool and guaranteed human progress, and progress itself became for many erstwhile biblically-oriented Americans a substitute for the eschatological vision of the kingdom of God.

All of this came together to form a kind of moral crisis immediately after World War II. At the center of the crisis was a well-intentioned, humane, intelligent piece of legislation, the G.I. Bill of Rights, which guaranteed all academically qualified veterans of World War II a college education. Leaving aside for now all the good things that came of it, two disruptive things happened as a result of this bill. First, the most able and intelligent members of the working class, the leaven of leadership which had always existed there, were removed and placed in the middle class, creating for the first time in the United States the beginnings of an underclass. Only the Black community retained a wide spread of leadership potential, since inferior segregated education had so radically reduced the capacity of Blacks as a group to enter college even with the G.I. Bill.

Second, the middle class was suddenly swollen with people who didn't know how to "be" middle class, who were constantly being moved or choosing to move as part of their upwardly mobile "career line." To the extent that these newly middle-class people found their experience difficult, the difficulty was caused by a kind of uprooting that led to a state similar in many respects to the "survival guilt" brought to attention in recent years by Robert Jay Lifton.

Many of those men who had followed the G.I. Bill route were suffering from straight survival guilt. They had lived through combat and four to seven years of academia to become well-paid and comfortable members of a new elite; many of them still survived on denial and psychic numbing. Others, with no combat experience, were nevertheless the first generation of their family to leave the close-knit extended family and neighborhood of the working class to be in intense competition with their peers at work. They, too, had left behind a life of social solidarity and bare material adequacy, like an old and trusted comrade, to become part of the new affluence. So there they were—all these people with college educations, well paid, with materially promising futures and all the security that car insurance, health insurance, Social Security, pension plans, and growing investments and home equity could provide. And a fair number of them were, as David Reisman put it at the time, part of a "lonely crowd," alienated, confused, and lacking in social identity.

A major issue was money. Some veterans thought that taking a G.I. home mortgage was immoral. They had vivid memories of the Depression and the wipe-out of their parents' entire fortunes and possessions through mortgage foreclosures and bankruptcy. "Going into debt" was immoral. However most veterans went for the mortgage and began to use credit to make a fast entrance into middle-class life, although they (and their wives) didn't do it without a sense of guilt and anxiety. Articles by psychologists began to appear in magazines, which explained how to identify what was causing credit anxiety and how to overcome it and become a "mature" consumer. Rapidly the whole matter of money and its use, the moral concept of "living within one's means," "meeting one's financial obligations," "paying one's bills punctually," "holding up one's side of the bargain," began to be far more flexible.

A mature "consumer" had complex strategies for dealing with money where no rules, no morality, only the law, obtained. To be able to make the transition from a working class, Depression-oriented, and rigid moral attitude towards money, to the perception of money as a kind of energy, a flow of power, which could be used to create whatever world or self one dreamed of creating, was regarded as evidence of a high level of psychological maturity. Morality really had no place in the great world of economics. Credit, and later the credit card, became a means whereby Americans were able to cushion themselves from reality. The credit card became a kind of key to life as pure process where issues of value no longer had much significance.

Philip Reiff has noted that a conscious, willed, acceptance of deprivation, what others have called delayed gratification, is an important part of culture. It is a way of organizing corporate life. Yet he notes also that there is a kind of cultural dialectic between deprivation and remission of deprivation. The sixties and seventies were a time of remission. Reiff regards that period as a time of movement into a remissive society, with the therapeutic paradigm, the "medical model," as a facilitator of the shift. To the extent that the church accepted the therapeutic culture, it too was a part of this facilitation.

The church, however, was hardly as powerful a facilitator of a remissive society as television. If you wanted to find out how to be an affluent middle-class person, television was quick to define the role—or life-style, as it began to be called. What to own, how to dress, where to live, where to travel, whom to associate with, what to talk about—the whole package was delivered by television. The nuclear family was the center; providing the "best" for the nuclear family was the sole moral dimension of the message. From Dick and Jane readers in the first grade to the endless sitcoms, moving in the seventies and eighties on into the soap operas, television described a world. First it was a world of aimless but accessible affluence, and then a dog-eat-dog world where the family, for all its hatefulness, was the only trustworthy social unit in a world determined to destroy the weak or foolish.

Americans, of course, did not swallow all this whole. How seriously individuals took it depended on many variables, including education, intelligence, mental and emotional stability, and religious commitment. Many parishes made a heroic attempt to provide an alternative ethos, a trustworthy community, but it was a great deal harder to stand against this assault than is generally understood. I would not hesitate to claim that church and synagogue members were less affected by this barrage of materialism and amorality than those who had no religious affiliation. Adult education classes, marriage counseling, whole church school curricula were used to resist it. Yet within the parish community itself a generally remissive atmosphere was cultivated, mainly to protect the self-esteem of people so constantly being reminded by T.V. that they might not be making it in the middle-class superbowl.

What morality was lost or changed as a result of all these forces, and what was the function of therapeutic theory in effecting this loss and change? In the transition from a life lived at a hard, subsistence level unbuffered by much domestic technology or mass transportation or easy credit, to the way we live now, what assumptions and behaviors were lost or changed?

During my own childhood, my moderately prosperous family bought its first radio, vacuum cleaner, electric refrigerator, washing machine (no drier), "Victrola," and, I believe, telephone. My first memory of a car is of a Franklin which regularly caught on fire and was equipped with a fire extinguisher. Other cars tended to have blowouts and break down with hair-raising regularity. Most roads had two lanes with bad shoulders. The top speed limit was forty. My father flew for the first time during World War II and I, for the first time, in 1960.

The middle-class values of this society were prudence, patience, fiscal honesty, sexual constancy in marriage, life-long marriage, hard work, keeping promises, modesty, telling the truth, patriotism, loyalty to friends, cheerfulness (never complain), responsibility of all adults for all children, a "good" education, sobriety (a surprising number of adults didn't drink at all during Prohibition) and democracy (treating tradespeople and servants with respect).

During my first eighteen years we had in our neighborhood the same mailman, neighborhood policeman, grocer, druggist, pediatrician, family doctor, school teachers, Episcopal minister, Roman Catholic monsignor, plumber, electrician, and garage mechanic.

During my first eighteen years I knew directly of one divorce; it was a neighborhood catastrophe. A number of my friends growing up died of diseases like pneumonia, scarlet fever, or polio, and all of us expected to get very sick from time to time. Morality was mightily buttressed by the absence of reliable birth control or safe abortion, the absence of transiency in the neighborhood, and the mutual assessment of character that went with this stability. We knew the surface behavior of each other very well.

Since most married women worked within the home, very few men could afford both to pay alimony and remarry. Middle class unemployment was a constant danger. Drinking was against the law until 1932, much feared by first generation middle-class people who saw it as a destructive working-class or upper-class habit. Salaries, even in terms of what they could buy, were low, and the moral obligations to save made them even lower. When savings reached a point where investment seemed prudent, property—that is, real estate—was regarded as wiser than the stock market. The very anemic cash flow in most middle-class families left very little time or opportunity for the social complexity of love affairs. Economic upward mobility was there, but it was for the most part slow and hard, tied to company or institutional loyalty, and not very competitive. Honesty and hard work were the best policy. Indeed the phrase "Honesty is the best policy" suggests that honesty is good because it works, and American morality during the first half of the twentieth century was blessed as much by a hard-headed pragmatism as it was by a biblical faith.

What have we lost? What has changed? Prudence. We often heard, and occasionally still hear, that risk is an important element in the Christian life. But risk most often meant risking one's psychological vulnerability, the display of deep feelings, or sharing intimate information about oneself and what one is "really" like. Somehow or other, risk and intimacy got mixed up together, and this led with inexorable emotional logic for many people straight to bed. The person determined to fulfill his or her human potential risked growth, risked throwing off old inhibiting habits and worn out ways of looking at the world to venture into new areas. This not only meant a new spouse, but also a new life-style with a new approach to money, perhaps a change in career, even a change in politics. The way all this was done was by a kind of leap of faith. The whole point was not to let a fear of consequences keep one from being liberated into the new age. The growing person would learn and grow even more from coping with the unpredictable consequences of new behavior.

However daring and attractive risk seen in this light may be, it is not prudent. Prudence, seen as a Christian virtue, is the awareness of limits that comes with the facing of one's creatureliness and mortality. It is perhaps the critical virtue needed to face the ecological crisis descending upon us. To ignore limits, to understand liberation as the denial of all limit, is the classical definition of *hubris*, fatal pride. The prudent person is suspicious of change without heed to consequence, of the belief that change, simply as change, is liberating.

Patience: "calmly to abide the issue of time; to suffer long without rage or discontent." This most neglected of virtues became nearly a vice from the sixties on. It got confused with passivity, which was regarded as pathology and tied to masochism. Before World War II, if one got sick one waited, patiently or otherwise, to get well. There was no penicillin. If you wanted to own your own house, you waited until you could afford to pay a fairly large proportion of the purchase price. A great deal of communication, business as well as personal, was by mail. The telephone was much used locally by the thirties, but a long-distance call was still an occasion for many middle-class people, and long distance calls were carefully monitored in business. The endless writing or dictating of letters and the slow putting together of corporate ventures by mail were an exercise in patience.

People became engaged when they intended to be married, but then there was often a long wait before the man could "afford to support a wife and family." The prudence in this arrangement required considerable patience as well—and of course when people grew old, their children made arrangements to take care of them. This *quid pro quo* between generations assumed patience as a high cultural value.

There is no need to go on. Perhaps no other value eroded so quickly. The punishing superego was seen as the father of patience. What possible reason was there to delay gratification in a world where what you wanted, according to TV, was always there to take. A favorite chant of the Woodstock generation was "We want it all! And we want it now!" The point of the chant was not to utter some eternal verity believed by that generation, but to cause as much pain and outrage as possible to the generation threatening them with Vietnam. No single statement could have been more outrageous to my generation than this assault on patience. Yet more than any Woodstocker could have believed or even intended, the attack on patience was successful. And the church was perhaps too agreeable to this moral retreat.

Parish ministers were the ones usually turned to when parents became too old to live alone. Middle-aged people with adolescent children, at the height of their careers but about to face college tuitions, were suddenly faced with elderly strangers, their parents, whom they had seen only occasionally over the past twenty years. These occasional visits had often been tense, even stormy, and the tension was usually due to conflicts of value — particularly in the raising of children. Now one or both of these parents were coming to stay, and their middle-aged harried children turned to the local pastor for advice.

In too many cases this pastoral encounter was *pro forma*. Both parties knew that the pastor's job was to alleviate the guilt of the couple as they planned some sort of economically viable elderly placement. Yes, the pastor would agree, it would not be good for the children to be submitted to conflicting theories of childraising. Yes, children find the irrational behavior of senescence disturbing, and it is hard for them to have their friends over. No, it would be a bad idea for the woman to quit her part-time job to care for this needy parent. She had a life of her own. (Nothing was said of the man's quitting his job.)

Often the elderly were themselves relieved by this decision, dreading the prospect of a dependent old age full of conflict and the hassle of children whom they barely knew and had no patience with. Again, the way our society was structured conspired against normal generational continuity and made any alternative terribly difficult. Yet it may be that the therapeutic assumptions that went into this kind of counseling made it too easy to choose placement. Parishioners who made this choice often felt considerable guilt, for all their pastor's reassurance, making it hard for them to visit their elderly

parents and resulting in serious depressions when parents
died. On the other hand, families who took their aged
parents in without even consulting their pastor, and did so
in a matter-of-fact way, usually found they could negotiate
some sort of viable relationship and created some sense of
continuity for their children, which was helpful to them in
making sense out of the world as adults.

Certainly sexual and economic patience ceased to be of
significant value in most mainline churches. A sexually
active adolescence became as common among Christians
as any other group; Christian adolescents are as addicted
to shopping with credit cards as anyone else. After all, the
pill, the diaphragm, and the money were there, at least for
the middle class.

Slowly women began to realize that the greatest
determining factor in setting their social role, the
inexorability of childbearing and child raising, was no
longer inexorable. The new domestic technology sharply
reduced the demands of "keeping house" and women
suddenly had the deciding vote on when or whether to
have children. It was a stunning freedom. Yet it was a
freedom for which there was no precedent, and no one,
woman or man, knew how to use it. Women no longer
needed men to "provide" for them, yet to be a "good
provider" had been the moral center of the middle-class
man's identity, his part in the sacred contract of
monogamous marriage. To be a good "home maker,"
which was the woman's role in a technologically primitive
society and a complex and demanding task with many
skills, became something any fool could do. Even men. In
their off hours.

Also unanticipated, and too often unnoticed, was the
new sexual competitiveness between women and men

that began in the jungle of adolescence. With sexual abstinence hardly a viable alternative, with the models of good providers and faithful husbands, good homemakers and competent mothers nearly vanished from the scene, physical attractiveness became enormously important in adolescent relationships between the sexes. "Looking good"—fit, thin, correctly dressed—being a "hunk" or a "fox," began to determine who won and who lost. Suddenly there were sexual winners and losers, hot performers and inept turkeys. Competition is inherent to the mating process, but it had been carefully regulated; now sex was a kind of biological game, a game with more losers than winners.

Few middle-class Americans today can emerge from adolescence able to trust members of the opposite sex or bring to the long-term relationships necessary for social stability or raising children much enthusiasm.

It is too early—and too reductive—to blame the destructive aspects of a sexually remissive culture on therapeutic theory or on "Freud," who would have been appalled by what we have. The therapeutic model for a healthy family has been as radically questioned by the sexual revolution as the Christian middle-class family. What therapists regarded as the biological determinism of maleness and femaleness was not that different from what the church believed had been determined by God, and feminists today are often even more angry at the psycho-therapeutic model than they are at the Christian one.

Classical therapeutic theory has always been a socially conservative force in its insistence on the strong family as the basis for mental health. The disintegration of the traditional family and the rise of feminism have caused more panic in the therapeutic community than in the church, mainly because the church has always had a tradition—though honored more in the breach—of seeing the parish household as a voluntary alternative to the very imperfect institution of the natural family. The parish household has a pastoral father, rather more like a mother, who dresses in sexually ambiguous garments on Sunday and whose time is more likely spent meeting the random needs of parishioners than efficiently scheduled to get things done.

The social role of the therapist today has been to make traditional middle-class morality more adaptive to techno-genic changes in society, chiefly the mindless and unanticipated changes that have caused such social turbulence and suffering. Assuming that the proper human response to change is always adaptation rather than resistance, therapeutic theory eased the letting go of traditional morality; it had little or nothing to say, however, about what should replace it or whether it should be replaced at all.

Where there are moral guidelines for our corporate life beyond those that empirically serve the "survival" of the most fit, where biology has largely supplanted culture, then the fear of death becomes the primary motivating factor in all human endeavors. In the past, particularly in classical Christianity, this motivation has occasionally been regarded as a necessary inhibitor of violent behavior, but the most untrustworthy of all motivations for the building of a moral world. The central social function of all religions is to build a culture which mitigates the fear of death, freeing its members from suspicion and fear of one another so that compromise, cooperation, and consensus can result in a moral and peaceful world. In this final section I shall offer some suggestions on directions the church, and particularly the parish congregation might take to begin building such a moral world.

A great many people in the United States, even those who are doing very well, sense that there is something wrong; the old ways are passing without any trustworthy new ways to take their place. Public radio and public television, two media that are less inclined to pontificate than to interview, allow people caught in social change to speak for themselves. On P.B.S. one hears farmers, stockbrokers, investment bankers, politicians, industrial workers, doctors, scientists, professors, high school students, with a very even selection of the sexes, talk about the world and about life as these affect their own world and their own lives. The common thread that runs through their testimony is a sense of fear, aggravated by the unpredictability and general untrustworthiness of our corporate life. The economy, the state of education, the state of public health, the state of the world ecosystem, geopolitics, sexuality, excessive litigation—this whole litany of national issues is seen not only as problems for which there are no solutions, but as issues for which there are no trustworthy moral guidelines, no moral criteria to help us live through them with hope and with some assurance that we are good people, not merely lucky or unlucky, winners or losers.

Some politicians, sensing this paralyzing unease, have taken to calling for a return to basics, the old values—and, with the television evangelists, to the old-time religion. All this nostalgia is tempting, particularly for people of my age, but I don't know of anyone who has ever returned to the good old days, because the good old days are gone.

As we reach the end of a century we have already reached the end of an era, and with it a world-view which served us well enough, but no longer serves us much at all. We are living in a kind of mean time. It is an interim period, like that of Moses and the children of Israel in the wilderness, a bit nostalgic for Egypt and its familiar captivity, frightened by the unfamiliarity and the unpredictability and danger of the wilderness, and with an increasingly dim view of the promised land as time goes by and it doesn't appear on the horizon. This has happened several times in history, and the church led by the Holy Spirit has found a kind of Mosaic vocation in providing an interim law and a bright and compelling vision to build hope for the future. It is time that the church retrieve this Mosaic vocation and vision, and work at building an interim moral community, a makeshift, tentative model for what a Christian moral world might be like in the future.

As has been said a number of times in this book, psychotherapeutic theory has been useful in helping us to let go of, or to sit loose to, those aspects of an older morality which no longer make sense to us. But it has also contributed to a rebirth of social Darwinism, where the goal of life becomes simply adaptation for survival. Someone has pointed out that the most self-defeating aspect of human beings is their capacity for adaptation to their surroundings. Surroundings, environment, milieu, are in process. They change. Often quickly and dramatically.

Many of us have, for instance, adapted to the principle of "mutual assured destruction" as the most dependable way to avoid nuclear war. As Joanna Macy in her now-famous article tells it, the inability to adapt to this principle depressed her and she went to a psychiatrist. She was depressed by the possibility of nuclear war, she told the doctor. Soon it became clear that the doctor was going to help her to find out what she was really depressed about, assuming that it was repressed and unconscious and had nothing to do with nuclear war. Presumably a healthy person could adapt to M.A.D. and focus on things about which something could be done on an individual and personal level.

Psychotherapeutic theory, then, is not helpful in building a moral world. As Don Browning says, its metaphors of intimacy, adaptation, health, wholeness, and natural selection do not recognize any need for us to regulate corporate norms of behavior. It assumes that all the regulation necessary is in our genes, even if the genes tend to regulate behavior by driving human beings to create better or worse, more or less adaptive, cultures.

Yet at the same time this way of looking at the world has provided us with a kind of interim social organization, aimed at the mitigation of conflict and based on such non-moral "goods" as prosperity, enlightened self-interest, and health. These are among the values of a pluralistic society. According to the logic of this view, pluralism is good because it leaves room for the widest range of personalities and "value systems" and provides a place for everyone to feel comfortable.

Understood as a transitional, temporary, makeshift mode of social organization, pluralism is a great deal better than nothing, and it is certainly better than a society structured by force. The major difficulty with pluralism is that it exists within a larger paradigm of social Darwinism, where tolerance becomes a mere social overlay on the deep struggle for supremacy among the personality types and "value systems" within a pluralistic society. Gary Hart's sexual values are no doubt shared by enough people so that they would not have become important if he had not been engaged in a highly competitive exercise —becoming president. Suddenly, behavior that is generally condoned in our pluralistic society was put forward by the press as reprehensible; Hart's political rivals were forced to call it so even though they saw nothing reprehensible in it beyond indiscretion.

Equally important is the failure of consensus in dealing with public issues. Many rural communities in New England, for example, cannot agree about sewage disposal. Those with their own leaching fields can't see why they should be taxed for the treatment of sewage from the more thickly populated center of the village, with its public school and its town offices and stores. Pluralism leads to the kind of social fragmentation where any action beyond immediate self-interest ceases to make sense.

On the level of ideology, pluralism just barely keeps single-issue groups from each other's throats. With such groups the issue beneath the issue is winning, although they may regard it as "surviving." They believe that they are fighting for their lives, or for the survival of all that is good and right and true in the world. We see church congregations riven in two as the fragile truce of pluralism falls apart. Pluralism is better than nothing, than the all-out war of all against all, but the logic of our present experience would plead that we can lead a humane corporate life for only so long without some deeper consensus about the essential issues of our life together. Pluralism is at best a stop-gap structure within which to begin building a new consensus. The vocation of the church at such a time is to provide the ultimate ground on which to build a new culture, to validate this culture and to give it authority. It is to begin, however tentatively, to build a moral world and to model it in some sort of makeshift community.

At the very heart of a vision of a just world for Christians lies the Eucharist. Whether we speak of *metanoia* or paradigm change, the alternative to the failing paradigm of American life, the hyperadaptive individual in a hyper-competitive world, is to be found in the radically different way of addressing reality which the Eucharist presents.

From the first collect, the Eucharist assumes that there is one God — a single reality for the entire world. Perhaps no idea is so in conflict with the thinking of pluralism. Pluralists insist that reality is a cultural concept, different for each culture, a creation of language that is itself a vehicle of description and communication so inadequate as to make the idea of a single reality absurd. Indeed, the humanistic psychologies tend to regard the idea of a single reality as a form of soft fascism. Everybody has a right to their own reality, to declaring what is real for them.

If there is one God, if there is a single reality, no matter how distorted our perceptions of this reality may be, it becomes radically important to know who this God is and so to discover a way of coming—at least partially—to understand and to live in the reality this God creates. In the Eucharist we discover this God in the Bible's revelation and in the act of communion as we receive the body and blood of Christ. In the process of all this we find the sacred narrative of the Old and New Testaments, the distillation of this narrative and its meaning in the Nicene Creed, and then an intense rehearsal of the narrative of Christ's death and resurrection leading to the communion itself, followed by a prayer of thanksgiving.

Given the way that we Americans have been taught to make sense out of life, this entire exercise seems irrational and archaic. It seems utterly unrelated to the only reality we have been taught to trust, the reality of that which can be researched and measured and quantified and dragged into a lab and set as a problem and solved. Yet millions of Americans seem to be under some compulsion to participate in the Eucharist, are willing to live with a kind of cognitive dissonance, caught between a way of thinking and living and working which they understand but distrust, and a form of worship which, in a curious way, they trust but don't understand.

A makeshift Christian moral community must be based on reality as it is defined eucharistically. To do this requires us to retrieve narrative and metaphor as a means of understanding. Without metaphor, all understanding is digital and reductionist, blind at all times to what is not directly in front of it. Metaphor gives us a context that is both orderly and full of wonder; narrative gives us continuity, purpose and hope. The trouble is that the narratives and metaphors of the Eucharist are so foreign to our usual way of thinking that many people either become literalists, insisting on their empirical reality, or trivialize them by regarding them as an aesthetically pleasing play of symbols.

But a sacrament is neither of these, nor is it a confluence of both. Instead, it is the place where, through worship, the creation is continually in mysterious encounter with the redemption and all is made new. There is, however, a sacrament prior to the Eucharist on which all Christian moral consensus must be based, and that is baptism. In baptism our created and embodied selves become conscious of their redemption in the body of Christ, the church, the community of the Eucharist and the resurrection. For the second theological consensus on which all Christian moral consensus is based is the fact that we are members one of another in the body of Christ — even where we don't agree in matters of morality. If we do not think of ourselves as ultimately bonded, there is no urgent reason why we should go through the pain and expense of energy and sacrifice required to build even a makeshift moral world. It is too easy to get up and leave the room when animated disagreement borders on ugly conflict. As in marriage, if the commitment is tentative, the *appearance* of agreement does well enough until the explosion of conflict leads to an inevitable split.

In parishes we seem to have no way to build a moral consensus around such issues as abortion, divorce, adultery, homosexuality, or the raising of children. We lack a theological consensus on such issues as how Scripture is to be interpreted, the significance of speaking with tongues, the place of politics in preaching, or the use of inclusive language in worship. The hyper-competitive environment of our disintegrating culture leaves us only debate as a way of getting to agreement, and debate gets us nowhere if compromise is seen only as losing and winning equated with bare survival. Even if some compromise is reached, as in resolutions coming out of church conventions or governing boards, very few people see why they should take such resolutions seriously if they don't agree or if the compromise doesn't "feel" good. If I'm not "comfortable" with it, why should I go along with it? In issues of highest intensity, such as the ordination of women in the Episcopal Church, merely ignoring some moral resolution may not be enough and only leaving the church altogether will do.

It is here that narrative and metaphor become helpful. In debate, there is no time or logical place to tell a story. Eyes glaze over. Contestants stare at the ceiling, tapping their toes, waiting for the story to be over. Yet stories can handle a good deal more complexity than the ideological and politically correct abstractions of debate. There is another way to deal with controversial issues, where what consensus does exist can be discovered and used as basis for more.

When taking part in council, Native Americans have a tradition where all present are invited to "say their piece." Everyone, without interruption, tells the story of how they came to be affected as individuals by the question under consideration. The results of using this model are surprisingly different from debate, where one listens strategically, looking for specific weakness and vulnerability. We tend to ignore anything said by an adversary that is not a threat or a weakness. Yet if we are not expected to respond directly to another, we can forget our own agenda and actually hear all of what another person is saying. Anxiety and hostility are remarkably reduced.

I have been in a group of Christians where homosexuality was discussed in this manner. Each person present took enough time to tell how they had learned about homosexuality, what they were told about it, how they first encountered it in another person, how their ideas from their first knowledge of and encounter with homosexuality shaped their later understanding of it. This order of narrative was not suggested, but simply grew out of the telling.

Each person had had a unique set of experiences. Some had had largely negative encounters. Others had known or worked with homosexuals whom they had liked and respected. Still others had had a more mixed experience, but all had had one experience in common. It was to have known well and respected someone — a college roommate, a colleague, a friend, a family member — who, to their utter surprise, had turned out to be gay or lesbian. In all cases it had been a powerful and moving experience. For some the shock of recognition had been followed by a rapid distancing or even a breaking off of the relationship. For others it had resulted in a total transformation of how they understood homosexuality as they worked through their relationship with the homosexual person. For others, nothing decisive resulted; the encounter was left unexamined, forgotten, only to be remembered in the group, many years later.

When all had said their piece, describing how they had been affected by the issue in their own history without blame, judgment or debate, they discovered that the common ground, the shock of discovery, was a fertile field for discussion. It was, in fact, like other shocks. The shock of discovering as a child that one's parents engaged in sexual intercourse and that one was oneself a product of this bizarre and unpleasant, or at least hilarious, act. Or the first experience of the death of a contemporary and the shocking, felt, at least momentarily understood discovery that one was oneself mortal. Or, as one member of the group said, whose "piece" had been short and guarded, it was like discovering that one was oneself homosexual, that what one might have held in scorn and contempt was precisely what one was. Someone else added that it was like the classical act of conversion, the shock of discovering that one was a sinner, a self-centered, blind, insensitive, fearful person obsessed with one's own survival, and the greater shock yet of discovering that one was also acceptable to God, that in this shocking discovery lay one's even more stunning salvation.

The narrative mode in which we all initially spoke our piece seemed to lead directly to the metaphorical mode of the discussion. The group came to no clear policy decision on homosexuality; instead, it put together in an easy and collaborative and participatory way a resolution on AIDS for the General Convention. The usual harsh disagreements and debates common to such an enterprise were, surprisingly, lacking.

The group had been deliberately formed to avoid the fruitless competition of debate. We had agreed that what we held in common through baptism was more significant than our differences. This agreement assumed a single reality, interpreted eucharistically, however distorted our private views of this reality might be by sin. For each of us the degree of distortion in how we understood the nature of homosexuality was understood to be subsumed in the given of human sin—with the ever-present possibility that it might be redeemed by grace. I have seldom experienced such high seriousness in any other task group. We took each other at our word.

This is not to suggest a method as a "solution" to the "problem" of consensus. Rather it is to suggest that a truly theological context should generate a non-adversarial method appropriate to Christian discourse. Endless empirical analysis does not generate consensus, but win-lose debate; it may be helpful in the hard sciences (although this is beginning to be questioned and will, no doubt, be debated), but is less than helpful in building a moral consensus.

As Dimitri says in Dostoevski's *The Brothers Karamazov,* "If people cease to believe in the immortality of the soul, then everything is lawful." When I first read these words as an atheist in college, I assumed that Dimitri (or Dostoevski) was thinking in terms of reward and punishment, of heaven and hell. I'm not so sure now. Sissela Bok once commented in a newspaper article on the true meaning of "All's fair in love and war" that when life is seen in purely biological terms, procreation and survival, then everything — lying, deception, violence — is lawful, or at least justifiable. If all value is subordinate to the highest value of survival, certainly everything that enhances survival is presented as lawful. In America this is too often regarded as being "realistic." It seems that there is a single reality underlying our pluralism, a kind of reductionist biology, the "higher law" Fawn Hall referred to in the Iran-Contra hearings as the justification for shredding documents.

Whether we believe in the immortality of the soul or the resurrection of the dead, as Christians we are given a place beyond survival from which to look at history. For most of us it is a most parlous and rickety platform on which to stand, and only on occasion does it give us much solid assurance. We see it used by zealots of the right to claim nuclear war as God's righteous judgment on the world as the true believers are caught up into heaven and the rest cast into the fire. The secular world, and indeed many Christians, see that doctrine as pure illusion, a dangerous illusion, eating away at humanity's will to survive. Yet when we move into the world of narrative and metaphor, and away from empirical reductionism, we discern it as a spirited power working in history.

With no transcendent place to stand, individuals, to the extent that they dare to reflect at all, may see themselves fighting for their own survival in a disintegrating culture. They can only hope that the fight will take place at an economic level that will provide them with some illusion of security. Yet from the perspective of the resurrection, it is possible by God's grace for us to discover in the surrounding chaos signs and portents of something new being born, a resurrection taking place, out of the death of the old culture. The deconstructionist tendencies of so many contemporary thinkers is simply despairing recognition; it mirrors the cultural disintegration around us. The deconstructionists go beyond Korzybski's observation on language that the map is not the territory, to say that the map is forced upon the territory to occupy and shape it at the whim of the mapmaker, who is simply whatever group is in power. In other words, how the narrative will be told and which metaphors will be selected is simply a function of power. Whoever wins the war gets to write the history. This is certainly true where the fear of death is regarded as the primary motivating force in all choices which involve a commitment. As St. Paul knew so well and said so clearly, to live under the sovereignty of death is to live under the rule of Satan.

Thus three issues must be addressed theologically in order to begin to build a moral world. They are generational discontinuity, unpredictability, and the inadequacy of language to define or express what goes on in the world. If human beings are not convinced that even their genes will survive to form a new generation, if they cannot with any assurance promise anything for a decade ahead, and if they have reservations about the adequacy of language to define a single, shared reality or even question the concept of reality itself, they will see no reason to take on the demanding work of building a moral world — even the tentative, makeshift moral microcosm of a humane parish community.

The church, of course, speaks to all three of these questions, but in a language that perhaps seems more trustworthy to us than the empirical language of the world. This may be the case simply because it is more obscure, less pretentiously concise, more open to association. It is a language that lends itself more to dreams and visions yet is anchored in the tangible, visible, durable reality of the sacraments — in water and bread and wine — and of the sacramental, the generous sense of space of church buildings, the divine focus of the altar, the exalted play of organ and choir, the serious, intelligent readers of the biblical narrative, the God-crazed preachers of the Word, the celebrating, thanksgiving priest in Eucharist.

All this is enough to help us begin to learn what it means to live beyond survival, to put survival in its place as we accept that we have a right to be here for reasons that go beyond our fitness to survive, and an obligation with this right to accept history with God's blessing as a home for human beings.

As for the world, we shall have little effect on it so long as we believe that we are responsible for its management and obsessed with its survival. Christianity is a backwater, not a part of the mainstream. We are not here to shape the world, but to let God use us for its transformation in God's good time. In the meantime, with the kind of liminal insight possessed by marginal people, we do participate in the world's narrative, sustained by our own narrative and metaphors, building humane makeshift models for the coming great sovereignty of God, as we wait patiently and thankfully for God's triumphal completion of history in justice and truth.

BIBLIOGRAPHY

Gregory Bateson, *Mind and Nature: A Necessary Unity* (New York: Dutton, 1979).

Don S. Browning, *Religious Thought and the Modern Psychologies* (Philadelphia: Fortress Press, 1987).

Northrop Frye, *The Great Code* (New York: Harcourt Brace Jovanovich, 1982).

John C. Harris, *Stress, Power, and Ministry* (Washington, D.C.: The Alban Institute, 1977).

Richard Hofstadter, *Social Darwinism in American Thought* (Boston: Beacon Press, 1944).

Reuel Howe, *Man's Need and God's Action* (Greenwich, CT: The Seabury Press, 1953).

Alasdair MacIntyre, *After Virtue* (Notre Dame, IN: University of Notre Dame Press, 1981).

Janet Malcolm, *Pysochoanalysis: The Impossible Profession* (New York: Knopf, 1981).

Peter Marris, *Loss and Change* (New York: Oxford University Press, 1960).

Cieslaw Milosz, *The Witness of Poetry* (Cambridge, MA: Harvard University Press, 1983).

Anders Nygren, *Agape and Eros* (Philadelphia: Westminater Press, 1953).

Bruce Reed, *The Dynamics of Religion* (London: Darton Longman & Todd, 1978).

Philip Rieff, *The Triumph of the Therapeutic* (New York: Harper & Row, 1966).

William Stringfellow, *A Private and A Public Faith* (Grand Rapids, MI: Eerdmans, 1962).

Watzlawick, Beavin and Johnson, *Pragmatics of Communication* (New York: W. W. Norton, 1967).

Joseph Weizenbaum, *Computer Power and Human Reason* (New York: W. H. Freeman, 1976).